# Evangelicals and Liberation Revisited

# Evangelicals and Liberation Revisited

An Inquiry into the Possibility
of an Evangelical-Liberationist Theology

João B. Chaves

Foreword by
Roger Olson

WIPF & STOCK · Eugene, Oregon

EVANGELICALS AND LIBERATION REVISITED
An Inquiry into the Possibility of an Evangelical-Liberationist Theology

Copyright © 2013 João B. Chaves. All rights reserved. Except for brief quotations in critical publications or reviews, no part of this book may be reproduced in any manner without prior written permission from the publisher. Write: Permissions. Wipf and Stock Publishers, 199 W. 8th Ave., Suite 3, Eugene, OR 97401.

Wipf & Stock
An Imprint of Wipf and Stock Publishers
199 W. 8th Ave., Suite 3
Eugene, OR 97401

www.wipfandstock.com

ISBN 13: 978-1-62032-785-2

Manufactured in the U.S.A.

In memory of Constâncio Luiz Chaves e Antonia da Silva.
Para sempre vivos na memória e no coração.

# Contents

*Foreword by Roger E. Olson* | ix
*Preface* | xi
*Acknowledgments* | xv
*Abbreviations* | xvi

1 The Problem: An Introduction | 1

2 Latin American Liberation Theology and North Atlantic Evangelicalism: Reaction and Renewal in Two Different Contexts | 14

3 Scripture and Hermeneutics | 36

4 Marxism, Socialism, and Violence | 49

5 Church, World, and Salvation: A Case Study on James McClendon Jr. and Gustavo Gutierrez | 70

6 Christology | 92

7 Post-Conservative Evangelical Theology: A Bridge between Evangelicalism and LALT | 105

8 Conclusion | 124

*Bibliography* | 131

# Foreword

THIS BOOK, BY BRAZILIAN theologian João Chaves, fills a gap in liberation theology literature as well as one in evangelical literature. To the best of my knowledge, no full length treatment of engagements between Latin American liberation theology and evangelical theology exists. In fact, up to date scholarly discussions of liberation theology have been hard to come by for some time. And evangelicals have by and large stood aside from liberation theology and, to their own detriment, I judge, attempted to ignore it.

A misconception about liberation theology has arisen. It is that liberation theology has fallen on hard times and there's nothing really new to say about it. Some celebrate that while others worry over it. Chaves very helpfully corrects that misconception and demonstrates that liberation theology is alive and well in Latin America. He brings to readers' attention some important recent developments in the field, including the works of some liberation theologians most North American students of liberation theology will probably not have heard about.

Most importantly, however, Chaves offers the only book length critical exposition and analysis of evangelical responses to liberation theology from the latter's beginning. Thus, his book serves several functions and all of them very well. Someone who wants a contemporary Latin American theologian's view of the history and development of liberation theology can find it here. Someone who wants the story of liberation theology brought up to date can find it here. Someone who wants to know what evangelicals have said and thought about liberation theology can find it here. Finally, someone who wants a Latin American evangelical theologian's view of liberation theology can find it here.

For a relatively brief book, *Evangelicals and Liberation Revisited* is comprehensive and at the same time insightful and critical. I benefited from reading it and have the privilege of knowing the author who has helped me

*Foreword*

understand and think both critically and sympathetically about liberation theology as only an insider, that is, a Latin American Christian scholar of liberation theology, can do.

Roger E. Olson<br>
Professor of Theology<br>
George W. Truett Theological Seminary<br>
Baylor University

# Preface

ONE OF THE MOST cherished memories of my childhood is that of my grandmother in the kitchen cooking and singing. She was a pious Pentecostal woman. But not like these tv-watching, make up-wearing, pants-dressing Pentecostals of today. She was a faithful member of a small, old-fashioned Assemblies of God church in Recife, Brazil. In the kitchen, she always sang her favorite song—or at least the favorite phrase of her favorite song—which she didn't mind repeating over and over, contemporary-worship style. If I think hard enough I can still hear her singing: "Sacred Bible, you are the light of my Brazil; you are the lance and the sword, of this courageous people."[1] Although I am tempted to criticize what I perceive as the song's unwarranted personification of the Bible, I celebrate the fact that my grandmother taught me to love Scripture and to use it as a tool to interpret reality. I never talked to her about her understanding of the song or how she thought the Bible could guide the people of Brazil, many of whom live in extreme poverty. I suspect, however, that she sang it in a "spiritual-eschatological" way; that is, in a way that understood Scripture to be valuable almost exclusively as a book that teaches the acrobatics of soteriological rewards. Nevertheless, I love the song—or at least my grandmother's favorite phrase of it—and strongly believe what it says: that the Bible is a distinct book that can light the way for those who read it faithfully and who are courageous enough to follow its teachings. As an evangelical, I gladly admit that the Bible speaks of salvation in the sense of "soul-healing." What I also admit, however, is that the guiding power of Scripture transcends the insider-outside dynamics that evangelicals have emphasized for so long.

This book calls evangelicals in general and conservative North-Atlantic evangelicals in particular away from a reductionistic view of their faith

---

1. The Portuguese lyrics to this song are: "Bíblia Sagrada, És a luz do meu Brasil, És a lança e a espada Deste povo varonil."

*Preface*

and towards the idea that, when it comes to using the Bible as a guide for living, Latin American Liberation Theology can be a fruitful dialogue partner. As a matter of fact, I will argue that evangelicals can be liberationists. Because of my own story—part of which will be told in the introduction—I took this for granted for some time, but I eventually realized that conservative evangelicals have reacted very negatively to liberation theology. When I moved to Texas, where I went to college and seminary, I realized that this negative resistance was even stronger among conservative *American* evangelicals. Furthermore, after reading the works of conservative evangelicals in the English-speaking world, I realized that the criticisms made by Latin American evangelicals of liberation theology are for the most part mere translations (and sometimes really bad ones) of works produced in the North-Atlantic. The fact that many if not most of the evangelical publishing houses that produce the resources used by evangelicals in Latin America are either heavily influenced by or dependent on literature and/or money that comes from conservative institutions from the English-speaking world makes it difficult to disassociate the North-Atlantic theological conservatism from that of Latin America. I chose to focus on these North-Atlantic evangelical responses to liberation theology partially because of their widespread influence and power.

Recently, I asked a relative to bring a few books on liberation theology from Brazil. When I received the books—all of which could only be found in Roman Catholic book stores— I was reminded of how stigmatized liberation theology is among conservative evangelicals. After giving me the books, my relative delivered a message sent by a Presbyterian minister who is highly respected by our family. The pastor wanted to tell me that Christians who get involved with liberation theology tend to leave their Christian faith behind. My relative, who by then seemed to be concerned with my soul's well being, looked puzzled by my response; I told her that instead of undermining my faith, liberation theology helped me become a better Christian. My hope is that this book will demonstrate how this is the case.

I also encountered resistance from non-evangelicals who, despite praising my desire to show the plausibility of an evangelical-liberationist theology, told me that this was an impossible task. I am sure some evangelicals agree with them, but those who think this way seem to suffer from a contagious condition: namely, the inability to appreciate the richness, heterogeneity, and dynamism of these two movements. If non-evangelical Christians and conservative evangelicals develop the interest and patience necessary to go through the pages of this book, it is my hope that, by the time they are finished, the former will be able to resist the temptation to see all evangelicals as social conservatives and the latter will be willing to awaken to the evangelical spirit latent in liberation theology.

To use the words of Brazilian singer Raul Seixas, the following pages are a petrification of an "ambulant metamorphosis"; that is, they are the product of someone's thought that is always improving or depraving. In many ways, this is intended to be a brief call for a re-conversation between two groups whose relationship "got off on the wrong foot"—and has remained severed ever since. I do not claim to present particularly original arguments here; I just attempted to fairly represent all parties involved. Constructive and potentially destructive criticism is welcomed, as is feedback that provides the opportunity for dialogue that facilitates my growth in knowledge and wisdom. Finally, it should be mentioned that this book was written primarily to students and practitioners. As such, I avoided the use of extensive and technical qualifications as well as copious footnotes.

# Acknowledgments

I would like to thank Professor Roger Olson. He was the one who encouraged me to submit this manuscript for publication. I appreciate his guidance and support both during and after my time as his student.

Dennis Tucker, Grear Howard, Cecilia Garcia, Kathryn Sublett, Rene Maciel, Javier Elizondo, Mary Ranjel, and Marconi Monteiro provided indispensable help during my time studying in the country of Texas. I am grateful for their help. If it was not for these people, life in this foreign soil would have been much harder.

Many people read parts of this manuscript and offered helpful criticism. Those who were aware that they were reading parts of this book include Maria Monteiro, Andrew Kim, Rick McClatchy, Nora Lozano, David Maltsberger, Linda Cross, Charles Comer, Josias Bezerra, and Victor Martinez. David Wilhite, Steven Porter, and Barry Harvey also provided helpful feedback on works that eventually made their way into this piece. The insights of these brothers and sisters made this work better, except for the parts where I stubbornly chose to ignore their advice.

My theological conversations with Mike Quinlan, Matt Hanzelka, James Hoskins, Daniel "Brokeback" Crowther, Luiz Ferreira, Rubim Barros, and Sergio Cruz helped me test liberationist ideas against evangelicals who happen to be in different points of the conservative/not-so-conservative spectrum. I am thankful for their patience and companionship.

Bill Walker was kind enough to use his editorial skills and experience to make my broken English more palatable. I have learned much from Bill's editorial remarks and from his theological knowledge.

I would like to thank my mother, Beijanete Bezerra da Silva, and my mother-in-law, Wanda F. Lima, for their patience and support.

Finally, I want to thank my wife Paula Chaves and my "little Americans" Jonathan Chaves and Rebecca Chaves for making life joyful and interesting. I love them much and they constantly remind me that I still have a lot to learn.

# Abbreviations

| | |
|---:|---|
| CEBs | Base Ecclesial Communities |
| CELAM | Conferencia del Episcopado Latinoamericano |
| FMC | Free Market Capitalism |
| ISAL | Iglesia y Sociedad en America Latina |
| LALT | Latin American Liberation Theology |
| NAEvs | North Atlantic Evangelicals |
| RCC | Roman Catholic Church |

# 1

# The Problem: An Introduction

## The Significance of Latin American Liberation Theology and the General Evangelical Attitude Toward It

DURING A VISIT TO New York in 2008, Honduran Cardinal Oscar Rodrigues Maradiaga was asked by interviewer David Gibson about the state of liberation theology. The Cardinal answered with a story about Fr. Gustavo Gutierrez. According to the Cardinal, during a conference in Mexico in 2006, Gustavo Gutierrez, one of the most important names associated with Latin American Liberation Theology (henceforth LALT), was asked whether the movement was dead. Gutierrez replied: "I don't know if it is dead. I was not invited to the funeral."[1] Gutierrez went on to say that "Eighty percent of liberation theology is the option for the poor, and this is alive."[2] This answer highlights a characteristic of LALT that has been pointed to not only by Gutierrez but also by other liberation theologians—namely, that LALT is not so much a movement as "a new way of doing theology."[3]

The fact that LALT has reached the end of an era as a cohesive movement, however, seems hard to deny. As David Tombs points out, while "individual theologians and communities in Latin America continue to positively identify themselves with liberation theology,"[4] LALT does not

---

1. Gibson, "Who Needs a Lifetime," lines 119–20.
2. Ibid., lines 121–22.
3. Gutierrez, *A Theology of Liberation*, 12.
4. Tombs, "Latin American Liberation," 30.

have the same impact it did in the 70s. Despite the apparent weakening of its cohesiveness, the diversification of liberation theology into a series of theological movements that share the liberationist ideological foundation is taken by theologians as evidence of its contemporary significance.[5] Furthermore, the liberationist method has been extrapolated into other cultures and religions as one can today find—beyond the well known black, Latin American, and feminist expressions—Jewish, Palestinian, Islamic, Confucian, African, Hindu, Buddhist, Asian, Queer, and even Deaf liberation theologies.[6] Mario Aguilar speaks about the diminishing visibility of LALT and presents another reason for the movement's perceived lack of cohesiveness. He says that

> It is to civil society, the world social forum, the ecological movement, the stop poverty campaigns, the movements for democracy and the overall saving of the planet that LT have turned to, in alliance with other partners in civil society. Thus, it could be argued that Medellin was the start of a liberation movement "within" theology and "without" theology that remains stronger than ever; however, those theologians seem not to be present simply because most of them work outside very traditional church structures imposed by John Paul II and Benedict XVI and that the alliances with civil society have made them more active but less visible in a Catholic theological world within a secularized and more evangelical Latin America.[7]

Therefore, the lack of cohesiveness and diminishing visibility of LALT as a movement does not necessarily mean that LALT has lost its significance and influence.

The widespread acceptance of the liberationist method among many Christian and non-Christian circles, however, was not reproduced among North-Atlantic Evangelicals (henceforth NAEvs) in general. Though the objective of LALT—namely, a more just world—was never challenged by NAEvs, its method and presuppositions were many times dismissed as misguided,

---

5. Nunez, "Relevancia y Pertinencia," 49.

6. For a sampling of liberation theologies in different religions see Miguel de la Torre (ed.), *The Hope of Liberation in World Religions* (Waco: Baylor University Press, 2008). One approach to queer liberation theology is given by Marcella Althaus-Reid in *The Queer God* (London: Routledge, 2003). For an example of deaf liberation theology see Hannah Lewis, *Deaf Liberation Theology* (Burlington: Ashgate, 2007).

7. Aguilar, "The Kairos," 28.

inefficient, and even heretical.⁸ Nevertheless, some evangelicals went beyond the acceptance of LALT's goals and incorporated some of its method into their own theologies. Ronald Sider and Clark Pinnock can be pointed to as examples of NAEvs who have accepted some premises of LALT's method.

Canadian Evangelical Ronald Sider, for instance, embraces the doctrine that Gutierrez claims as the central teaching of liberation theology: namely, the preferential option for the poor. Sider says that "one of the central biblical doctrines is that God is on the side of the poor and the oppressed."⁹ For Sider, it is evangelical theology that risks heresy if this teaching is not incorporated. Writing over a decade after the conception of LALT, Sider affirms that "evangelical theology has largely ignored this doctrine, and thus [its] theology has been unbiblical—indeed even heretical—on this important point."¹⁰ Clark Pinnock, whose work will be addressed in greater detail later, affirms LALT's understanding of God's call for politically active obedience. Pinnock says that "the Bible offers politically relevant criteria that need to be injected into the process of planning and governing."¹¹ This biblical criteria is in line with the liberationist, socialist approach, because "(s)o long as the desire for profit motivates the world economic system, the needs of the poor cannot be met. Such a system serves only those who can command resources and enter into the market as purchasers."¹² Therefore, Pinnock agrees not only with LALT's articulation of the necessity of active political involvement, but also with its discourse on oppression, exclusion, and on the need for the implementation of socialistic policies.

---

8. NAEvs generally agree with the goals of LALT, but not with its means. Humberto Belli and Ronald Nash argue that, as a system, LALT relies on bad economics and theological heresy. For more see Huberto Belli and Ronald Nash, *Beyond Liberation Theology* (Grand Rapids: Baker Books, 1992): 55–56. W. Dayton Roberts, in an article that appeared in Christianity today in 1979 entitled "Where has Liberation Theology Gone Wrong?," argues for the intrinsic incompatibility between LALT and Evangelicalism. Kenneth Hamilton, in one of the earliest collections of essays dealing with LALT from an evangelical perspective, affirms not only that the means of LALT are inappropriate but also that "That liberation theology is a heresy I believe to be beyond question." See Kenneth Hamilton, "Liberation Theology: Lessons Positive and Negative," in *Evangelicals and Liberation* edited by Carl Armerding (Phillipsburg: P & R Publishing, 1977). The above mentioned examples are not exceptions among evangelicals, but characterize the general approach of NAEvs toward LALT.

9. Sider, "An Evangelical," 314.

10. Ibid.

11. Pinnock, "A Call," 136.

12. Ibid., 135.

## Evangelicals and Liberation Revisited

Examples of positive interaction between the two movements, however, are limited in number and influence. Sider shared the optimistic expectation that

> ... in the coming years millions of us evangelicals will allow the biblical teaching that God is on the side of the poor and oppressed to reshape fundamentally our culturally conditioned theology and our unbiblically one-sided programs and institutions.[13]

This expectation, however, remains unrealized. His call for a "truly evangelical theology of liberation that will alter the course of history"[14] remains mostly unheard among evangelicals of different persuasions. The fact that the term "evangelical," though applicable to Christians who represent a wide variety of theological beliefs, is still usually associated with the "religious right" of the United States is an indication that the preferential option for the poor was not embraced by evangelicals in general. A number of evangelicals, however, are still attempting to develop an articulation of Evangelicalism that takes the challenges presented by LALT seriously.[15] This book is an effort toward a similar direction. It is a modest attempt to argue for the possibility of an authentic evangelical-liberationist approach to the Christian Faith.

## The Author's Location

As religion theorist Thomas Tweed pointed out, theories are "sightings from sites. They are positioned representations of a changing terrain by an itinerant cartographer."[16] I am convinced that theories are not trans-locative,

---

13. Sider, "An Evangelical," 318.

14. Ibid.

15. Though recent publications by NAEvs that reflect significant evangelical-liberationist interaction are limited in number, direct evangelical engagements with LALT and with themes that are central to LALT are still being published in English. For Examples see Mary Elizabeth Berry, Peter Goodwin Heltzel, and Bruce Ellis Benson (eds.), *Prophetic Evangelicals: Envisioning a Just and Peaceable Kingdom* (Grand Rapids: Wm. B. Eerdmans Publishing, 2012);Bruce Ellis Benson and Peter Goodwin Heltzel, *Evangelicals and Empire: Christian Alternatives to the Political Status Quo* (Grand Rapids: Brazos Press, 2008); Sharon Heaney, *Contextual Theology for Latin America: Liberation Themes in Evangelical Perspectives* (Colorado Springs: Paternoster, 2008); and Ronald J. Sider, *Rich Christians in an Age of Hunger: Moving form Affluence to Generosity* (Nashville: Thomas Nelson, 2005).

16. Tweed, *Crossing and Dwelling*, 13.

## The Problem: An Introduction

so I acknowledge the necessity of identifying my location. This is so that the reader can be reminded that though I will attempt to say something to everyone, this "something" is said from somewhere specific. Identifying my location may help readers recognize my "horizon of interest" or the "ideology"[17] that underlies my thinking. Indeed, one is never conscious of all the ways in which one's location influences one's thinking. Nevertheless, there is value in allowing the reader to be aware of the place from which I see things. Doing so enables the reader to better judge whether my arguments are fair to those I oppose and whether I positively expand the view of those who do not share my location in turn.

I was born in a non-Christian household during a time when my native Brazil was under the last stages of a right-wing military dictatorship. It wasn't until I was a preteen that I had the "evangelical experience" when my grandmother took me to church. My parents never became confessional Christians. At the same time, having been raised by loving non-Christian parents made it difficult for me to make sense of the sharp separation between "those of the world" and "the saints of the church." Part of the problem was that my parents, who by the definition of my evangelical mentors were regarded as lost and "of the world," were many times more Christ-like than the "saints of the church" that I knew. Defining a "saint" by using the language of "forensic justification" or "imputed righteousness" that comes at the moment of explicit confession of faith in the name Jesus made little sense to a boy like me who had inherited much of his father's skepticism. A sharp distinction between church and world, therefore, was never acceptable.

Growing up thereafter in an evangelical Baptist church was an interesting experience. Even though Brazil was going through major political changes during my adolescence, politics was treated as primarily a private

---

17. "Ideology" here is used as a neutral term; for liberation theologians what deems any given ideology good or bad is the goal to which it is subordinated. Liberation theologians, however, are not univocal in the use of the term "ideology." Leonardo Boff, for instance, uses the term "ideology" in a neutral way but never defines it. See Leonardo Boff, *Passion of Christ, Passion of the World: The Facts, the Interpretation, and the Meaning for Yesterday and Today* trans. By Robert Barr (Maryknoll: Orbis Books, 1987): 1. It is clear, however, that he sides with Jose Miguez-Bonino and Juan Luiz Segundo in his use of the term. Bonino defines the term as "a system of representations which have an existence and a historic role in a given society"; for Segundo, ideologies can be understood as the systems of goals and means that serves as the necessary backdrop for any human option or line of action. For additional information see Jose Miguez-Bonino, *Toward a Christian Political Ethics* (Philadelphia: Fortress Press, 1983) and Juan Luiz Segundo, *The Liberation of Theology*, trans. by John Drury (Maryknoll: Orbis Books, 1973).

matter, and political allegiances were, to my knowledge, never publicly admitted. Sermons and Sunday school classes focused on being "spiritual," which meant that concern for this world in the form of historical action was only understood to function as a tool for accomplishing what "really mattered." At home, I witnessed my father's work assisting politicians of different competencies. Traveling with my parents to political rallies opened my eyes to the organizing power of politics. .

It was also during my adolescence that I read my first book on politics—Marx's and Engels's *The Communist Manifesto*. After reading this book, which I understood only partially, I—still blinded to the evils of the totalitarianism of the left—became convinced that communism was the Christian's political position of choice. Che Guevara and Fidel Castro were next on the list, both of which I read before the age of 17 and before becoming aware of the existence of something called "liberation theology." I did read Leonardo Boff during the same years but never connected Boff to any particular theological movement. Despite Boff's continuous affirmation of the need for contextuality, his arguments sounded like obvious, straight-out-of-the-bible Christology to me. Needless to say, this unsophisticated teen did not see any explicit contradiction between the teachings I received from my evangelical mentors and the often Marxist-influenced teachings of liberation theology. As far as I could tell, the two approaches seemed more complementary than contradictory.

Since this time of course, the potential conflict between evangelical theology (a disputed term that will be tentatively described below) and LALT has become more pronounced. As mentioned above, the goals of LALT were never the issue, but LALT itself was seen by my evangelical mentors as an enemy rather than an ally. Some of that antipathy was caused by uncritical anti-Catholic feelings, a common phenomenon in a place where the Catholic majority found creative ways of suppressing the "evangelical threat"; however, significant doctrinal matters were also at stake. Those mentors failed to recognize that LALT had ecumenical beginnings, and that Catholic liberation theologians were fairly distanced from the Catholic majority.

This dual appreciation for evangelicals and liberationists has been a part of my journey almost since my introduction to Christianity. As an evangelical, a high-view of Scripture, a sense of conversion experience, engagement in spiritual disciplines, and participation in enthusiastic forms of corporate worship are an integral part of my understanding of the Christian

*The Problem: An Introduction*

life. However, as someone who found in LALT answers to questions that were not even being asked in the evangelical circles of which I was a part, I found in LALT an approach that could actually strengthen my evangelical commitments. Investigating whether evangelicals can be liberationists, therefore, finds a place within my own story. As such, while I will approach the topic as critically and objectively as possible, the nature of the motivation that gave rise to this modest and brief investigation is personal.

## Why Revisit The Evangelical-Liberationist Interaction?

An argument for the possibility of an evangelical-liberationist theological approach can take many forms. The great majority of the evangelical articulations that have tried to implement the positive achievements of LALT into their own approach, however, have been variations of the same strategy: that is, the acceptance of liberationist teachings that do not threaten what is usually perceived as doctrines and political tendencies that help "define" what it means to be "evangelical." One way of implementing the gains of liberation theology into evangelical theology is arguing against the socialist tendencies of the former by defending the conviction that true liberation can only be accomplished in a free market system and therefore avoiding the problems that may arise because of LALT's use of Marxism.[18] Another, more common way is looking at LALT as a heresy that helps evangelicals re-think the general direction of their commitment to evangelical convictions.[19]

---

18. For an example of this approach see Humberto Belli and Ronald Nash, *Beyond Liberation Theology* (Grand Rapids: Baker Book House, 1992). Belli and Nash argue that the solution for Latin America's economic stagnation is a new religious-Christian morality combined with the implementation of an effective Capitalist system. For them, Latin Americans have a culture of low productivity, lack of responsibility, poor compliance with standards, and lack of punctuality. The issue of poverty, therefore, is not properly addressed by LALT, whose economic analysis fails to consider the cultural factors that ultimately keep the majority of Latin Americans in poverty.

19. Theologian Kenneth Hamilton, for instance, argues that LALT is a heresy that "is forcing us to re-examine the meaning of orthodoxy." The way in which LALT helps "re-examine" orthodoxy, however, is not by helping arrive at answers that challenge previously held convictions but by providing new questions that must be answered in ways that do not require previous convictions to be significantly re-thought. For further information see Kenneth Hamilton, "Liberation Theology: Lessons Positive and Negative," in *Evangelicals and Liberation*, edited by Carl Armerding (Phillipsburg: P & R Publishing, 1977): 120–127; and Kenneth Hamilton, "Liberation Theology: An Overview," in *Evangelicals and Liberation*, edited by Carl Armerding (Phillipsburg: P & R Publishing, 1977): 1–9.

Evangelicals and Liberation Revisited

I will attempt to use a different approach as I will re-visit instances of the evangelical-liberationist interaction re-examining the generally suspicious response given to LALT by NAEvs. But why revisit that specific interaction? It is my conviction that the response that LALT received in the North Atlantic in general—and by North Atlantic evangelicals from English speaking countries in particular—are deficient for several reasons out of which two stand out. First, a number of influential evangelical theologians who responded to LALT failed to take into serious consideration the fact that both Evangelicalism and liberation theology are considerably heterogeneous and dynamic movements. Secondly, there is a significantly limited interaction between these two movements in light of new developments in both evangelical theology and LALT.

The failure of NAEvs in accounting for the heterogeneous, dynamic nature of the two movements caused two main problems that have been left unresolved:

1. By attempting to present "the evangelical" response to LALT, NAEvs alienated distinct forms of Evangelicalism.
2. Secondly, by providing rigid characterizations of LALT, NAEvs failed to see how close some forms of LALT can be to some expressions of evangelical theology.

Furthermore, the limited contemporary interaction between the two movements may have been partially caused by the great number of evangelical responses that characterized the two movements as intrinsically opposed. Evangelicalism and LALT could have already been characterized in ways that would highlight their proximity rather than their distance during the time when evangelicals where still actively responding to LALT (late 70s to early 90s). Recent developments in both movements, however, opened possibilities for developing even stronger arguments for such proximity. Examples of these two major failures in evangelical responses to LALT will be briefly explored below. It is my intention that, as this book progresses, such failures become increasingly clear.

## Failure in Seriously Considering the Diversity and Dynamism in Both Evangelical Theology and LALT

Writing for *Christianity Today*, one of the most influential evangelical magazines in the world, evangelical theologian W. Dayton Roberts affirmed that "the two systems, liberation theology and evangelicalism, are not really compatible."[20] Roberts, however, never defined either Evangelicalism or liberation theology as he either intentionally or not positions himself as a spokesperson for evangelicals in general. Among Roberts's concerns is his belief that LALT does not leave room for "the positive place of suffering, martyrdom, and the 'cross' in Christian experience."[21]

Roberts's concern, however, is not shared by evangelicals who agree with many of the criticisms made by theologians such as Leonardo Boff and Jon Sobrino regarding the detrimental social consequences that the traditional christological images of suffering servant and powerless baby can have in the Latin American context.[22] Roberts also fails to take elements of Boff's Christology into account as Boff makes a strong case for the necessity of imitating Christ in his giving of his own life to others, a lifestyle that Boff considers to be a form of martyrdom.[23] Furthermore, theologians of different traditions have recognized a few Latin American liberation theologians as martyrs both before and after Roberts's article. Colombian priest Camilo Torres and Archbishop Oscar Romero are probably the best known examples of such "liberationist martyrs."

Roberts's inability—or unwillingness—to offer a fair account of either Evangelicalism or LALT is not the exception among North-Atlantic evangelical responses to liberation theology. Many of such responses come across as reductionistic articulations of Evangelicalism, LALT, or both. Raymond Hundley, for example, argues that only theologies that espouse revolutionary violence should be considered true LALT.[24] Such an affirmation would immediately alienate theologians who are considered founders of the movement such as Leonardo Boff and Dom Helder Camara. Furthermore, Hundley ar-

---

20. Roberts, "Where has Liberation," 1401.

21. Ibid., 1400.

22. Samuel Escobar and Rene Padilla are examples of evangelicals who are sympathetic to the liberationist criticism of the use of traditional images of Christ in certain context. For a clear account of the issue see Sharon Heaney, *Contextual Theology for Latin America: Liberation Themes in Evangelical Perspectives* (Colorado Springs: Paternoster, 2008): 160–62.

23. See Leonardo Boff, *Jesus Christ Liberator: A Critical Christology for Our Times* (Maryknoll: Orbis Books, 1978): 219–20, 223, 247, and 255. Boff also makes the point that life must be lived as a sacrifice (martyrdom) for others in his book on Christology that was published after Robert's article. For additional information see Leonardo Boff, *Passion of Christ, Passion of the World: The Facts, The Interpretation, and Their Meaning for Yesterday and Today*, trans. by Robert Barr (Maryknoll: Orbis Books, 1987): 63 and 94.

24. Hundley, *Radical Liberation*, 35.

gues that it is impossible for an evangelical to join the liberationist movement due to the evangelical commitment of the authority of Scripture. For him, one cannot join such movement unless the authority of the Bible is denied because the Bible condemns revolution.[25] Most evangelicals, however, have a high-view of Scripture and, at the same time, are not willing to affirm that the revolution that freed the United States from British domination was a flagrant disobedience to God's will. Anyone who has participated in an evangelical Fourth of July service knows this. Therefore, in trying to establish clear boundaries between LALT and Evangelicalism, Roberts and Hundley, who are but two examples of the general evangelical approach to LALT, exclude significant representatives of both persuasions. As this work progresses, I will attempt to make more of these reductionisms explicit and to build an argument for the compatibility of both approaches.

## Limited Contemporary Interaction Between Evangelical Theology and LALT

The great majority of works dealing with LALT from an evangelical perspective were written, as mentioned above, between the late 70s and early 90s. Since then, new developments in both evangelical theology and LALT have been introduced. Nevertheless, to my knowledge, no major attempts to study the relationship between these movements in light of such developments have been made. Among the developments in LALT one can mention Jung Mo Sung's articulation of a form of socialistic society that acknowledges the necessity of a market and Ivan Petrella's understanding of liberation theology as a theology that has as its central function the development of historical alternatives to neoliberalism.[26] Among evangelicals, Roger Olson's introduction of the concept of Post-Conservative Evangelicalism is, in my opinion, one of the most significant developments. For Olson, Evangelicalism can be best characterized as a centered, not as a bounded-set movement.[27] Below, I will consider these and other developments as potential bridges between Evangelicalism and LALT.

---

25. Ibid., 23–24.

26. See Jung Mo Sung, *Desire, Market, and Religion* (London: SCM Press, 2007) and Ivan Petrella, *The Future of Liberation Theology: An Argument and Manifesto* (Burlington: Ashgate Publishing, 2004).

27. Olson, *Reformed and Always Reforming*.

*The Problem: An Introduction*

## Strategy and Objectives

The strategy that I will use in this book will be threefold. First, I will present a critical reading of selected evangelical responses to LALT. These responses will be divided into 4 chapters (from chapter 3 to chapter 6) and will focus primarily on the central characteristics of Evangelicalism as identified by David Bebbington: biblicism, activism, conversionism, and crucicentrism. I will present and assess these responses in light of liberationist and evangelical perspectives and/or insights that may have been excluded. This will be done as an attempt to highlight the deficiencies of evangelical reactions to LALT. Finally, I will conclude with an argument for the use of new developments in both movements as a path that opens up the possibility of an evangelical-liberationist position. As already implied above, my objectives are highlighting the reductionistic tendencies of the responses of NAEvs to LALT and suggesting pathways for fruitful contemporary interactions between evangelical theology and LALT.

## Summary of Chapters

At the outset of their award winning work on twentieth-century theology, Stanley Grenz and Roger Olson state that "Theology describes faith within a specific historical and cultural context, and therefore it is unashamedly a contextual discipline."[28] Because I share this conviction, I will present a brief history of both Evangelicalism and LALT. Being aware of the historical situation out of which any given theology is constructed allows for a better understanding of the theological and practical concerns that give specific flavor to the doctrinal convictions held by believers. This history will be the subject of chapter 2. Though a detailed account of the historical development of either Evangelicalism or LALT is not the purpose of this piece, chapter 2 will present the reader with some of the major historical events and experiences that helped shape the ever changing identity of these movements.

Chapter 3 will deal with the issue of the understanding of Scripture and hermeneutics in evangelical theology and LALT. The chapter will start by presenting the criticisms made by prominent NAEvs to LALT's use of Scripture and to its hermeneutical method. The first part of the chapter will focus on the responses given by a few influential evangelicals, then, challenges to the conservative evangelical approach to Scripture and

---

28. Grenz and Olson, *20th Century Theology*, 9.

hermeneutics from both LALT and the evangelical tradition will then be given. In this chapter, the author will attempt to suggest that the conservative evangelical approach to Scripture and hermeneutics is defective and, therefore, liberationists are warranted in their opposition to such an approach.

Bearing the title "Marxism, Socialist Society, and Violence," chapter 4 will start with the evangelical criticisms aimed at LALT's use of Marx's social analysis and its endorsement of a socialist society. I will also present the objections that NAEvs raise against LALT's general support of violence. The challenges to such criticisms will come from a proper assessment of LALT's use of Marx, from Jung Mo Sung's criticism of the absolutization of the market system, and from an analysis of the relationship between American evangelicals in general and just war theory. With this chapter I will attempt to show that, in general terms, NAEvs have misunderstood the relationship between LALT and Marxism; furthermore, by presenting Mo Sung's criticism of free market Capitalism, I will attempt to show readers how sectors of LALT have articulated forms of socialist-like tendencies that, while maintaining some of the utopia that characterized the early stages of LALT, are not unrealistically optimistic regarding the effectiveness of historical options that advocate complete rupture with any form of market system. Finally, by showing the close connection between evangelicals in general and just war theory, I will show the inconsistency that haunts American evangelicals who criticize LALT's generally accepting position in regards to revolutionary violence.

The relationship between church and world will be dealt with in chapter 5. Soteriological matters will also be discussed in the same chapter. When it comes to the relationship between church and world, I will compare two influential works on systematic theology, namely, James McClendon Jr.'s *Ethics* and Gustavo Gutierrez's *A Theology of Liberation*. McClendon's volume was chosen for two reasons. First, it is a respected systematic theology written from the perspective of the Free Church Tradition, which is the tradition to which I belong. Secondly, McClendon's separatistic tendencies position him on the opposite extreme of Gutierrez in the "church-world relationship spectrum" while maintaining his evangelical identity. Gutierrez's work was chosen because it is a faithful representative and praiseworthy articulation of LALT's position regarding the way in which church and world should interact. Soteriology will be discussed in connection to the issue of church and world for both issues are, as I intend to argue, closely connected.

*The Problem: An Introduction*

Chapter 6 will present the Christology of Leonardo Boff, which is representative of the general LALT approach to the life and work of Jesus Christ, and argue that the potential tensions between Boff's Christology and evangelical Christology can be resolved if Boff's work is appropriated as complementary rather than contradictory to the general evangelical approach. Presenting Roger Olson's articulation of Post-Conservative Evangelicalism and the positive evangelical responses to LALT is what chapter 7 is about. The book will be concluded in chapter 8, where I will summarize the findings of this research and attempt to present my final argument for the possibility of an evangelical-liberationist approach.

# 2

## Latin American Liberation Theology and North Atlantic Evangelicalism: Reaction and Renewal in Two Different Contexts

THE WEALTH OF RESOURCES dealing with the historical developments within both Evangelicalism and LALT is considerable.[1] This chapter is neither an attempt to challenge or replace existing insights into these movements' development nor an effort to present a significantly different reconstruction of the history of these movements. Instead, this chapter's aim is to emphasize the dynamic and diverse character of such movements that is often neglected by partisan accounts of them. Because the focus here will be on the changing phases of both Evangelicalism and LALT, names and dates will be kept to a minimum. After presenting a brief account of both movements, I will conclude by arguing that

1. Both Evangelicalism and LALT are closer today than they were a few decades ago and

1. For examples of good historical accounts of LALT see *The Church in Latin America: 1492–1992* edited by Enrique Dussel (Maryknoll: Orbis Books, 1992); David Tombs, *Latin American Liberation Theology* (Boston: Brill Academic Publishers, 2002); and *Liberation Theology: A Documentary History* edited by Alfred T. Hennelly (Maryknoll: Orbis Books, 1990). For examples of historical accounts of Evangelicalism see Rob Warner, *Reinventing English Evangelicalism, 1966–2001: A Theological and Sociological Study* (Colorado Springs: Paternoster, 2007); David Bebbington, *Evangelicalism in Modern Britain: The Age of Edwards, Whitefield and the Wesleys* (Downers Grove: Intervarsity, 2003); Douglas A. Sweeney, *The American Evangelical Story: A History of the Movement* (Grand Rapids: Baker Academic, 2005); and Roger Olson, *The Westminster Handbook to Evangelical Theology* (Louisville: Westminster John Knox Press, 2004).

2. Despite their differences, both movements began with a reaction to the perceived need for reform and renewal in the religious reality that dominated their specific context.

## LALT: A Reaction Against an Oppressive Context

Reacting against the strong focus on divine transcendence that characterized the Western theological development of the 1960s, the theologies of liberation arose committed to bringing Anglo-European theologians down from their "ivory towers." These new theologies also wanted to respond to the diverse experiences of oppression that existed in the contexts in which they were developed and that were being neglected by what they perceived as the highly speculative thought of both traditional and North Atlantic theology.[2] LALT, unlike other liberation theologies that arose in the 60s, was developed in the only continent that is simultaneously Christian and poor.

Most historians agree that LALT came into being in the second half of the 1960s. During that time, a historical context of hope, optimism, and struggle for social change spurred the simultaneous development of liberation theologies around the world.[3] Writing in the 70s, the late Yale University historian Sydney Ahlstrom argued that the rise of a "technocratic society" during the 60s, which was marked by massive urbanization, influenced the whole world. According to Ahlstrom, as technological and demographic developments led to both an urban and a radical crisis, historic religious convictions and loyalties were being challenged.[4] The *aggiornamento* of Vatican II, which represented a significant endorsement of more progressive thought among Catholics, combined with the possibility of conceiving a world without hunger brought by the advances of the 60s, played and important part in the development of the Latin American liberationist approach—which addressed what Latin American theologians considered to be the greatest evil in their environment—namely, poverty.[5] The postwar Catholic Action movement, Karl Marx's social analysis, political theologians such as Jürgen Moltmann and Johannes Metz, and even the Cuban Revolution are also part of the complex heritage of LALT.

---

2. Grenz and Olson, *20th Century Theology*, 200–201.
3. Witvliet, *The Way of the Black Messiah*, 3.
4. Ahlstrom, "The Radical Turn," 1–9.
5. Witvliet, *A Place in the Sun*, 24.

Evangelicals and Liberation Revisited

Liberation theologians from Latin America recognize their indebtedness to Western theology, politics, and philosophy; however, they broke away from the traditional Western mindset significantly.[6] According to LALT, the *theologia perennis* developed in Europe cannot properly address the issues that arise in the Third World, as any theology tends to support the praxis out of which it is developed.[7] Hence, pre-commitment to a specific context is seen as inevitable. Uruguayan theologian Juan Luiz Segundo makes this clear when he says:

> In Latin America, literally millions of people are dying because for five centuries the gospel has been interpreted in a particular way. [. . .] (In Latin America) the gospel is read in a way that kills not only the Christian who reads it, but real persons who die because others have interpreted the gospel in a particular way.[8]

Thus, LALT challenges the biblical exegesis that predominated in most of the twentieth century and avoided the political questions implicit in Scripture by promoting a split between a devotional reading, practiced by the congregations, and a historical-critical reading, practiced by the academy.[9] The approach taken by LALT, consequently, takes a "pre-theoretical" first step[10] as its commitment to the process of liberation precedes any theological reflection.[11]

## From the 60s to the 80s: Foundation and Development

It is not uncommon for Western theologians to consider the Second Vatican Council to be the most important event in the life of the movement that came to be known as LALT.[12] Though Vatican II was indeed

---

6. Moylan, "Denunciation/Annunciation," 38–40.
7. Bevans, "Models of Contextual Theology," 185–86.
8. Segundo, *Signs of the Times*, 119.
9. Gorringe, "Political Readings of Scripture," 74.
10. Phan, "Method in Liberation Theology," 57.
11 Witvliet, *A Place in the Sun*, 24–25.
12. Stanley Grenz and Roger Olson consider Vatican II to have "opened the doors to radical social and political involvement by Catholic laity and clergy" (Grenz and Olson, *20th Century Theology*, 211); Alister Kee characterizes Latin American Liberation Theology a "post-conciliar movement" (see Alister Kee, "The Conservatism of Liberation Theology: Four Questions for Jon Sobrino," in *Political Theology* 3 [2000]: 36); Andrew Kirk, who wrote one of the first Evangelical responses to the movement also portrays LALT as

significant, radical movements were brewing inside the Roman Catholic Church before the council convened.[13] This is especially true of LALT, a movement that has its early and ecumenical beginnings often forgotten by North-Atlantic theologians.

According to Raymond Hundley, LALT has its roots in a movement born nine years before the famous meeting of Medellin. This movement, called ISAL,[14] was a primarily Protestant movement that operated under the auspices of the World Council of Churches. According to Hundley, Rubem Alves, a Presbyterian minister from Brazil, was the first theologian to publish a work of LALT as an identifiable movement. His dialogues with Gustavo Gutierrez, who is often considered the father of the movement, influenced the Peruvian priest significantly.[15] Brazilian Catholic Theologian Jung Mo Sung agrees with Hundley as he points to Alves's doctoral dissertation entitled "Towards a Theology of Liberation" (1968) as the movement's foundational work. According to Sung, Gutierrez's work may be considered paradigmatic for being the most systematic of the movement's foundational period, but it was not the first.[16] Leonardo Boff, who also points to ISAL as a major force in the foundational period of the movement,[17] argues that the beginning of LALT can be traced back to the base ecclesial communities (henceforth CEBs). According to Boff, the CEBs started in the mid 50s, when Dom Angelo Rossi responded to the lack of priests by using lay catechists to lead ecclesial communities. By 1963, two years before the ending

---

being made possible by Vatican II (see Andrew Kirk, *Liberation Theology: An Evangelical View of the Third World* [Atlanta: John Knox Press, 1979]: 24). Such approaches seem to overlook the historical situation of Latin American Christianity before Vatican II.

13. In the context of Europe, one can point to many Catholic thinkers who dialogued creatively with Marx before the council. A few examples are: Emanuel Mounier (1905–1950) who dialogued with Marxism much before John XXIII's papacy. The Nouvelle Theologie dialogued with Marx as did theologians and students at the Catholic University of Louvain, which was a center for dialogue between Christianity and Marxism in Europe. For more examples of radical Catholic movements in Europe that preceded Vatican II see Malik Tahar Chaouch, "Cristianismo y Politica en America Latina: El Paradigma de la Teologia de la Liberacion," in *Desafios Bogota* 17 (2007): 160–165. In Latin America one can point to Paulo Freire, a Catholic thinker whose influence started to be felt in Brazil as early as the late 50s, and to the work of Dom Angelo Rossi, who started lay-led ecclesial communities that already practiced a form of liberation theology in the early 60s.

14. ISAL stands for *Iglesia y Sociedad en America Latina*, which means "Church and Society in Latin America."

15. Hundley, *Radical Liberation*, 4–9.

16. Sung, *Teologia*, 67–73.

17. Boff and Boff, *Introducing*, 69.

of Vatican II, social action was already the central focus of the CEB gatherings. According to Boff, the episcopal meeting in Medellin that is often seen as the event that allowed LALT to exist within Roman Catholic communities only gave "citizenship right" to these groups where some form liberation theology was already being practiced.[18]

Despite the ecumenical and diverse nature of LALT, due to the fact that during the early stages of liberation theology Latin America was overwhelmingly Roman Catholic, theological treatises written by Roman Catholic thinkers made greater impact than those written by Protestants; consequently, the movement became primarily "Catholicentric."[19] Additionally, the fact that the Roman Catholic Church (henceforth RCC) is considerably more structured than any Latin American Protestant institution makes it significantly easier to trace the developments of LALT in connection to Latin American Catholics. In light of this fact, a convenient historical marker for the start of the liberationist movement in Latin America is the publication of Gutierrez's work, *A Theology of Liberation* in 1971. Though, as we saw above, Gutierrez's work is not the first of the movement, it was received as the conclusion of the movement's period of early development.[20] Gutierrez's work, therefore, represents the consolidation of LALT as a cohesive, sophisticated movement.

If the date and the specific Christian orientation from which LALT arose are unclear, the same is true of its characteristics. Though many theologians are eager to label LALT as being necessarily Catholic, Marxist, and pro-violence, such characterization only works as a vague generalization. Rubem Alves, whom many consider to be the movement's true founder, was Presbyterian; Jose Comblin heavily criticized Marxism and all kinds of hegelianisms since the 1960s;[21] and Leonardo Boff and Dom Helder Camara were pacifists. Ascribing Roman Catholicism, Marxism, or violence as necessary components of LALT reduces the diversity that characterized the movement since its beginnings. Therefore, the features that characterize early LALT must be broad enough to account for this diversity.

Methodist liberation theologian Claudio de Oliveira Ribeiro recognizes the characteristics that make LALT unique without compromising the diversity that characterizes the movement. He provides a list of five

18. Boff, *Eclesiogenesis*, 9–10.
19. Ribeiro, "Teologia é no Plural," 97.
20. Dussel, "Recent Latin American," 394.
21. Assmann and Sung, *Deus em Nós*, 111.

features of LALT that accounts for the general principles of the movement in its early stages without falling into the reductionistic tendencies mentioned above, which are:

1. The praxis of the liberation of the poor.
2. The acknowledgement of the necessity of a scientific analysis of social reality.
3. The conscience of the socio-economic dependence of theology and of the church.
4. The understanding of theological reflection as a tool for social transformation.
5. The central place of economy in theological reflection.[22]

A significant number of works from the liberationist perspective were published in the 1970s. In addition, organizations such as Christians for Socialism in Chile were actively involved in bringing the social changes advocated by LALT.[23] The socialist policies that were advocated by LALT and the organizations that embraced it, however, would not for the most part be successful in Latin America. The leftist movements in the continent would be met with great resistance from the ruling elites of Latin America. Talking about the turbulent context of Latin America in the 1970s, David Tombs says:

> During the early 1970s, Brazil positioned itself as regional policeman. The Brazilian military successfully exported their National Security ideology to neighboring militaries in the Southern Cone and Bolivia. Military coups in Bolivia (1971–1978), Chile (1973–1989), Uruguay (1973–1985), and Argentina (1976–1983) ensured that in the 1970s and 1980s, almost the entire continent was under dictatorial rule.[24]

The military regimes in Latin American were largely supported by the United States of America, a fact that influenced early works of LALT into erroneously characterizing external factors as the sole cause of Latin America's underdevelopment.

In the 1970s there were many conservative Latin American Bishops who openly opposed LALT. Though the Vatican's official position toward

---

22. Ribeiro, *A Teologia*, 29.
23. Tombs, *Latin American*, 137–38.
24. Ibid., 159.

liberation theology was to a great extent still unclear during the decade, conservative Bishops were appointed to key leadership posts in Latin America as the Vatican's attempt to diminish the growing influence of LALT in the continent.[25] The appointment of Alfonso Lopez Trujillo as secretary general of CELAM in 1972 was probably the most significant case of conservative leadership among Latin American Catholics.[26] If during the 1970s the Vatican was ambiguous in its position in relation to LALT, the first half of the 1980s saw the intensification of the resistance against LALT as the Vatican by then explicitly resisted LALT in many ways.

The most significant demonstration of such resistance was manifested in two documents published by Joseph Cardinal Ratzinger, then the prefect of the Congregation for the Doctrine of the Faith. The first, published in 1984, was entitled *Liberation Theology*; the second, published two years later, came to be known as *Instruction of Christian Freedom and Liberation*. In these documents, Ratzinger criticizes LALT of being reductionistic for reducing the Christian liberation to a temporal one[27] and for adopting not only Marxist social analysis, but also its strategies for solving the problem of poverty.[28] Jose Comblin criticizes Ratzinger for erroneously convincing John Paul II that the main problem in Latin America was Marxism and that LALT and the CEBs indoctrinated the people into Marxist thinking.[29] McGovern argues that Catholic critics of LALT such as Ratzinger many times confused the populist movements that were influenced by LALT (such as Christians for Socialism) with liberation theology, and consequently erroneously ascribed the shortcomings of such movements to LALT itself.[30]

In the second half of the 1980s, changes in the social, political, and theoretic camps affected LALT significantly. Speaking about this period, Jung Mo Sung argues that five changes can be pointed to as central:

1. The abandonment of dependency theory by social scientists.
2. The crisis of the socialist bloc, which weakened Marxist social theories.
3. The rising and strengthening of other social struggles that showed some of the theoretical insufficiencies of LALT.

25. Petrella, "Introduction: Latin American," xiv.
26. Tombs, *Latin American*, 192–94.
27. Adulante, "La Doctrina Social," 307–8.
28. Ratzinger, "Liberation Theology," 367–70.
29. Comblin, *Quais os Desafios*, 60.
30. McGovern, *Liberation Theology*, 10–11.

4. The advance of radical post-modernity with its tendency to disqualify any discourse of politico-structural transformation in society.

5. The acknowledgement of LALT's difficulty in facing and solving fundamental theoretical problems.[31]

For Sung, it was during the mid 80s that liberation theologians in Latin America recognized the need of developing an articulation that paid closer attention to gender, cultural, and ethnic questions.[32] The inadequacy of LALT in general to provide satisfactory answers to these challenges had weakened the influence of the movement in Latin America considerably by the end of the 1980s.[33]

## From the 90s to Today: The Period of Crisis

What came to be known as the "period of crisis" in LALT started with the fall of the Berlin Wall in 1989. The fall of the wall was widely perceived as the definite victory of Neoliberalism over Socialism, an idea that presented the main challenge to LALT due to the movement's inability to point to any system other than Capitalism as a realistic historic alternative since.[34] This event did not mean that LALT had failed, but it did demonstrate how political and economic assumptions had changed since the 1960s.[35] Nevertheless, one can find strong evidence of LALT's influence in the 1990s. Some examples of this influence are: the election of Jean-Bertrand Aristide

---

31. Sung, *Cristianismo*, 44–45.

32. A famous example of such self-criticism can be found in Gutierrez's introduction to the 1988 edition of *A Theology of Liberation*. In it, Gutierrez points to the necessity of expanding the meaning of poverty so that it includes aspects of gender, culture, and ethnicity. He also acknowledges the inappropriateness of dependency theory, a theory he endorsed in the first edition of the book (see Gustavo Gutierrez: *A Theology of Liberation: History, Politics and Salvation* [Maryknoll: Orbis Books, 1988]: xxi–xxv). The Boff brothers also recognize the importance of accounting for other aspects of poverty/oppression. They are, however, somewhat dismissive of the matter as they consider "class oppression" to be "infrastructural" and other kinds of oppression to be "superstructural" and thus prioritize economic oppression over any other kind (see Leonardo Boff and Clodovis Boff, *Introducing Liberation Theology* [Maryknoll: Orbis Books, 1987]: 29).

33. Tombs, "Latin American Liberation," 47.

34. The fall of the Berlin Wall arguably represented the victory of Neoliberalism over alternative forms of social organization. This was a major problem for LALT because of its generally anti-Capitalist stance.

35. Tombs, "Latin American Liberation," 48.

in Haiti; the 1994 revolution in Chiapas, Mexico under the leadership of Samuel Ruiz, author of *Biblical Theology of Liberation*; and the indigenous rebellion in Ecuador influenced by Leonidas Proano, a liberation theologian, also in 1994.[36]

However, this period of crisis is in many ways still present today, as liberation theologians from Latin America respond to this new reality in different and, so far, inconclusive ways. Argentinian theologian Ivan Petrella points to three approaches to the reality presented by the perceived victory of Neoliberalism—three general responses that, according to him, suffer from a common defect: the inability to develop concrete alternatives to the current social idea of a historical project. He labels such responses:

1. Reasserting core ideas.
2. Revising basic categories.
3. Critique of the idolatrous nature of Capitalism and Modernity.[37]

The response that Petrella labels "reasserting core ideas" is an attempt to disassociate LALT from any particular socio-scientific mediation or historical project and to focus on features that have taken a more prominent role among liberationists since the 80s, such as spirituality and the preferential option for the poor. Gutierrez and Sobrino are mentioned by Petrella as examples of such an approach. Critics of LALT have argued that it is dishonest for liberation theologians to suggest that spirituality was central to the movement from its conception;[38] however, a careful reading of early works written by Latin American liberationists show that spirituality was seen as a foundational feature since the beginning of the movement.[39] Another feature of this response is its emphasis on the need for LALT in a world where inequality is on the rise. Petrella does not challenge the arguments presented by this response, but he does find them inadequate for ultimately giving up on emphasizing the need for a concrete historical project.[40]

36. Nunez, "Relevancia y Pertinencia," 50.
37. Petrella, *The Future of Liberation*, 2.
38. Belli and Nash, *Beyond Liberation*, 27.
39. Writing in 1980, Leonardo Boff considers theology to rise from spiritual encounter with the Lord amidst the poor (Leonardo Boff, "The Need for Political Saints," in *Cross Currents* 30/4 [December 1980]: 369). Gutierrez also considers spirituality to be central to LALT already in the first edition of *A Theology of Liberation* as he sees a close connection between spirituality and the process of liberation (see Gustavo Gutierrez, *A Theology of Liberation* [Maryknoll: Orbis Books, 1973]: 204–5).
40. Petrella, *The Future of Liberation*, 2–5.

The second response, "revising basic categories," accepts the above mentioned position but goes beyond it as it attempts to reformulate aspects of early LALT, such as the focus on revolution, the idea of the poor as history's driving force, and the concept of capturing state power. Pedro Trigo is the best known theologian put into this category by Petrella. The overly optimistic hopes that Trigo has for civil society, however, are pointed out by Petrella as the major shortcoming of this approach, which he also considers to be misguided.[41]

The third approach listed by Petrella has in Franz Hinkelammert its most famous figure. This response focuses on the critique of the idolatry that is perceived by liberation theologians in defenses of Free Market Capitalism (henceforth FMC) and Modernity. An idol, liberationists who hold on to this approach argue, is a god to whom life is sacrificed; therefore, their argument goes, Capitalism and Modernity are idols since they take priority over human life. For Petrella, this response fails because by pointing to the idolatry of Capitalism without giving a specific alternative, theologians who hold onto such an approach make Capitalism a necessary idol.[42]

Petrella's own alternative, an argument for the centrality of the task of constructing historical alternatives to Neoliberalism, is primarily a change of direction. Petrella, though helpful in his insights regarding the use of newly developed social theory, also fails in giving a reliable historical alternative to the political-economic-cultural system that declared victory with the fall of the Berlin Wall.[43] Therefore, he is a victim of his own criticism of the other approaches as there is in his own approach a similar inability to devise concrete, specific alternatives to the current dominating system. Petrella's insistence that liberationists need to construct historical projects is an interesting suggestion; however, his failure to recognize liberation theologians who have successfully done so shows that the effect of the fall of the Berlin Wall signifies LALT's inability of devising concrete alternatives to Neoliberalism.

As mentioned above, the challenges that came with the perceived victory of Neoliberalism are still very much present, and LALT is being shaped by them as it tries to develop responses that are adequate to the current situation. As a new generation of liberation theologians comes onto the theological scene, new concepts are inevitably developed—as every generation sees differently from its historical perspective. Therefore, the new

41. Ibid., 5–7.
42. Ibid., 7–11.
43. Ibid., 107–8.

generation of LALT cannot be analogous to the theology developed in the 60s and 70s; their respective situations are worlds apart. Besides the issue of the perceived victory of Neoliberalism, which seems to be the most prominent challenge, many other changes in the context with which LALT must interact are being taken into consideration by this new generation.

First, the reality of the development of LALT in the 60s and 70s was mostly rural; the new generation focuses on a mostly urban context[44]. Secondly, because the "Medellin Generation" saw inequality as necessarily immoral, they developed a static economic concept. The new generation can see the world in a more dynamic way in which it is acceptable to find ways to generate wealth. The new LALT is more comfortable with suggestions that involve the market, though not in any way close to a Capitalist use of the market.[45] Ribeiro argues that "Thinking theologically today, especially in solidarity with the poor, means seeking light on how to build community life in the context of Neoliberalism."[46] Sung agrees as he thinks that LALT has been unreasonably rigid in its economic analysis and suggests that notions of economic efficiency and competitiveness cannot be discarded.[47] These two examples show how liberation theologians in Latin America have developed approaches that are more nuanced than those of their predecessors when it comes to socio-economic factors.

Another important change in the Latin American context is the rise of Protestantism in general, and of Pentecostalism in particular. Berryman suggests that LALT needs to become "less Catholic" and that the new generation must cooperate with Protestant and Pentecostal churches.[48] The perception that LALT and Latin American Pentecostalism are in opposition,[49] however, finds exceptions in Brazil, by Pentecostal pastor

44. Berryman, "La Generacion," 81–82.
45. Ibid., 82–84.
46. Ribeiro, "Has Liberation Theology," 305.
47. Sung, *Desire, Market, and Religion*, 107.
48. Berryman, "La Generacion," 85.
49. For examples that imply some sort of opposition between the two movements see Jose Comblin, Quais os Desafios dos Temas Teologicos Atuais (Sao Paulo: Paulus, 2007): 60. Comblin regrets John Paul II's conservatism and the inability of LALT to thrive that resulted from John Paul II's conservative stance as a main reason for the rise of Pentecostalism. Samuel Escobar points to the rise of Pentecostalism among the poor as evidence of LALT's inability to mobilize the poor (see Samuel Escobar, "A Missiological Approach to Latin American Protestantism," in *International Review of Mission* [April 1998]: 170). Henri Gooren argues that it was the emphasis on literacy and study, the repression from military forces, and the pressure from the Vatican that eventually caused the migration of

## Latin American Liberation Theology and North Atlantic Evangelicalism

Ricardo Gondim—one of the most well known Christian personalities of the country who studied under Jung Mo Sung and is sympathetic to the liberationist agenda. In February of 2012, it was Gondim's Pentecostal mega-church that hosted the release party of the new edition of Rubem Alves's first book on LALT. Ed Rene Kivitz, a Baptist minister who is also a major Christian personality in Brazil, studied under Sung as well and does not see LALT as a threat. Though the friction generated by the competition for the religious demand between Protestants of different persuasions and Catholics does indeed cause some tension between them, the examples above show that the perceived opposition between Catholic liberationists and Protestants/Pentecostals is not necessary.

It is clear that there are many challenges to LALT that still need to be addressed. No system is without its shortcomings. But as the brief overview above has attempted to show, characterizing LALT based on the movement's foundational works, a popular strategy among critics of LALT, inevitably fails to consider the responses that liberationists gave to the changes in their contexts. LALT is a heterogeneous, dynamic movement and must be treated as such. From its inception, this theological approach claimed to be contextual and a theology of the signs of the times. To limit it to a specific, superseded context is not only to misunderstand its form, but also its nature.

## The Evangelical Movement

Recently, Rob Warner pointed out that one in every five Americans calls himself or herself an evangelical and two in every five claim to be born again.[50] In years of presidential election, the "evangelical vote," if such a thing exists, is prized by the candidates, as the support of evangelicals carry a lot of weight particularly in the southern states. Interestingly enough, the "evangelical vote" in the 2012 presidential election favored the Mormon candidate over the Christian one, a phenomenon that is already a testament of the dynamism of Evangelicalism even within its most conservative manifestation. It is precisely the dynamism together with the diversity

---

the poor from the CEBs to Pentecostal churches. If he is right, the migration of the poor from the CEB to the Pentecostal churches was caused primarily by sociological rather than theological matters (see Henri Gooren, "Catholic and Non-Catholic Theologies of Liberation: Poverty, Self-Improvement, and Ethics Among Small Scale Entrepreneurs in Guatemala City," in *Journal for the Scientific Study of Religion* 41/1 [2002]: 30–31).

50. Warner, *Reinventing English Evangelicalism*, 1.

that characterizes the evangelical movement that the historical overview below attempts to emphasize. Apart from the description of the pietistic and puritan influence on Evangelicalism, the history of the movement will be presented in roughly five stages:

1. The Great Awakening.
2. The Second Great Awakening.
3. The rise of Fundamentalism.
4. Neoevangelicalism.
5. The development of Post-Conservative Evangelical Theology.

Because this work focuses primarily on the response given by English speaking evangelicals to LALT, I will focus solely on the development of Evangelicalism in English speaking countries in general and in the United States and England in particular.

## The Use of the Term "Evangelical"

Mapping Evangelicalism is no less complex than attempting to define LALT. As in the case of the latter, Evangelicalism is heterogeneous, dynamic, and its central claims have developed considerably over time. The meaning of the word itself is contested, and its application varies from place to place. The usage of the word "evangelical" can be so multi-faceted that different definitions of its meaning can even contradict each other. According to its etymology, "evangelical" means "of the good news," but etymologies are often barren, conveying at best the broadest possible hint of a word's meaning. Defining "evangelical" broadly, however, may not be a bad strategy given the diversity of ways in which the word was and is used. In his book *The Westminster Handbook to Evangelical Theology*, Roger Olson identifies seven different ways in which the word "evangelical" has been used.

First, Olson points to the etymological meaning. As mentioned above, "evangelical" means "of the gospel," a definition that implies that "*Evangelicalism* is simply synonymous with authentic Christianity."[51] Evangelicalism, in this sense, is the Christian movement that proclaims salvation by faith alone through Christ alone.[52] Secondly, the word "evangelical" is

---

51. Olson, *Westminster Handbook*, 3.
52. Ibid.

used in connection to the sixteenth century Protestant Reformation.[53] In the European context, it is common for the word "evangelical" to be used as synonymous with Protestant. Another historical use of the word "evangelical" is to be found in Anglican/Episcopal circles. It refers to the party within Anglicanism that resisted those within the Church of England who sought to strengthen the Roman Catholic elements of their church.[54]

The Pietistic-revivalist effort toward reforming and reviving German, British, and American Protestant Christianity in the eighteenth and nineteenth centuries is also referred to as "evangelical." The call for Christian orthopathy by the pietists and the emphasis on conversionism by the leaders of the Great Awakenings are the main characteristics of the Evangelicalism of this period. The fifth use of "evangelical" identified by Olson is practically synonymous with the term "fundamentalist." In this sense, the term is used to identify the conservative group that reacted against the perceived threat of liberal theology, especially during the 1920s and 1930s.[55] The group of neo-fundamentalists that remained conservatives but distanced themselves from the militant fundamentalism beginning in the 1940s is identified by Olson's sixth use of the term "evangelical." The seventh use of "evangelical" is popular instead of scholarly and is used to identify any enthusiastic, militant, and highly conservative Christian group.[56]

The wide variety of the usage of the term "evangelical" makes giving specific definition to the term a nearly impossible task. Engaging in defining the meaning of this widely contested term is beyond the focus of the present work; therefore, I will adopt Olson's descriptions and will, unless otherwise mentioned, use the term "evangelical" to refer to the neo-fundamentalists described by Olson's sixth use of the term. In this chapter Olson's fourth and fifth use of "evangelical" will also be adopted as they historically precede and, for the most part, develop into the sixth use.

---

53. Ibid., 4.
54. Ibid.
55. Ibid., 5.
56. Ibid., 6.

Evangelicals and Liberation Revisited

## From Its Pietistic and Puritan Roots to Its Post-Conservative Articulation

### Pietism and Puritanism

The two major influences on what would come to be known as the evangelical movement are British Puritanism and Continental Pietism. The first was born in sixteenth–century England as a reaction to the perceived exaggerated influence of Catholicism on Queen Elizabeth's Protestant arrangement.[57] The three main general characteristics of this group that sought to "purify" English Christianity were the emphasis on the importance of preaching as the exposition of biblical content, the insistence on the observance of Sunday as the Christian Sabbath, and their focus on experiential Christianity—that is, the understanding of saving faith as a personal experience that authenticated one's status as Christian.[58] Though the Puritans did enjoy a time of influence in Britain, they ultimately failed to implement the reforms for which they fought. Nevertheless, some convictions held by the Puritans were shared by a few who separated themselves from England's state church and would eventually play a major role in the Great Awakening.[59]

The Pietistic movement was also a movement for reform and renewal in the Church. Continental Pietism began in the second half of the seventeenth century within German Lutheranism through the work of Phillip Spener and August Francke, his disciple. Their primary concern was revitalizing the Lutheran Church, whose emphasis on orthodoxy was perceived by them as strangling the need for orthopathy.[60] From Pietism, the evangelical movement would inherit its emphasis on personal piety and its fascination with conversionist soteriology.[61]

Unknowingly, Francke would have a great impact in what would be known as the Great Awakening. In 1722, Ludwig von Zinzendorf, a student of Francke, would invite a group of Moravian refugees to live in his estate. This community soon developed into a refuge for other Protestant sects who lived in some kind of ecumenical partnership.[62] It was through the

57. Sweeney, *American Evangelical*, 30.
58. Ibid., 31.
59. Ibid., 33.
60. Dillenberger and Welch, *Protestant* Christianity, 123.
61. Olson, *Westminster Handbook*, 12–14.
62. Sweeney, *American Evangelical*, 36–37.

mission-minded ministry of the Moravians that one of the most influential persons of the Great Awakening, John Wesley, was converted.[63]

## The Great Awakening

The Great Awakening, which peaked in the 1740s, was a revivalist movement in Britain and in the United States that was characterized by a considerable amount of ecumenicity and cooperation. It is to this period that the birth of Evangelicalism as a distinctive movement is usually traced. During this period, collaboration between a never before seen number of Protestant leaders was forged in the name of the work of evangelization. Leaders from different traditions worked interdenominationally and across geographical areas helping one another organize a series of corporative events.[64] Itinerant preaching, a common feature of this movement, helped not only the spread of the gospel but also the relativization of the zoning system that had helped keep the division among different Protestant sects for so long.[65] Three of the better known names connected to this period are John Wesley, George Whitfield, and Jonathan Edwards.

Despite the general ecumenicity seen by the Great Awakening, diverging groups were formed within the movement as well. Four of the most prominent of such groups were the New Lights, Old Lights, Old Calvinists, and Edwardsians. With the disestablishment of state churches, such divisions were furthered by the rise of several evangelical denominations. By the end of the eighteenth century a number of denominations had been successful at securing their share in the religious market.[66]

## The Second great Awakening

The Second Great Awakening came as a reaction to the perceived threat of Enlightenment into post-revolution United States. This was also a diverse movement which reached its peak in the second-to-third decades of the nineteenth century and in which evangelicals of different persuasions participated in gospel proclamation and cultural engagement. The cultural

---

63. Ibid., 37.
64. Ibid., 29.
65. Ibid.
66. Ibid., 56–61.

and social impact of Evangelicalism during this period was remarkable as evangelicals were deeply involved in fueling education, special needs institutions, missions, and even temperance reform.[67] Some of the major names associated with this period are Timothy Dwight, Charles Finney, Alexander Campbell, and Peter Cartwright.

## The Rise of Fundamentalism

The threat of liberal theology especially due to the influence of Darwinism and higher criticism began to be felt by evangelicals in the early nineteenth century. In reaction to this threat a number of evangelical scholars developed a form of evangelical theological approach that came to be known as fundamentalism. A good and concise description of the characteristics of fundamentalism is given by Humphreys and Wise in their book *Fundamentalism*. According to them, there are nine central characteristics to what they call generic fundamentalism:

1. It has religious origins.
2. Its adherents are traditionalists who retain aspects of their tradition selectively and, because of such selectivity, they may be faced with situations where their opponents are more faithful to the tradition they claim to protect than themselves.
3. It is a reaction against aspects of modernity.
4. It is a reaction against modernity for the specific reason that modernity is perceived as a threat to their personal and corporate identity.
5. It is a reaction against modernity that is manifested as a fight against it.
6. It is characterized by authoritarian male leaders.
7. The present is seen as a time of crisis.
8. Its adherents distinguish themselves by using definite boundaries that clearly differentiates between insiders and outsiders.
9. Its goal is to replace modernity with its own religious system.[68]

All the above characteristics are, to a varying extent, true to the fundamentalists of the early nineteenth century. However, an important

---

67. Ibid., 74–75.
68. Humphreys and Wise, *Fundamentalism*, 10–14.

qualification must be made. Unlike the fundamentalists of the 1920s, the early fundamentalists were not militant or separatistic.[69] Their goal was to reform the mainline denominations to which they belonged such that these denominations would not let go of what they perceived as Protestant orthodoxy.[70] Because of their defeat in accomplishing such reform and due to historical developments that they perceived as revealing a conflictive relationship between them and the general culture, including the mainline churches of which they were a part, some of these fundamentalists withdrew from the former denominations they failed to reform and became ultra-conservative.[71] It is to these "second-stage" fundamentalists that Humphreys's and Wise's characteristics better apply.

Another characteristic of these second-stage fundamentalists worth mentioning was the reaction to the social gospel movement. Because of what fundamentalists perceived as the overemphasis on the social aspect of Christian work in the teachings of the social gospel movement, they became less interested in the kind of social reform in which they were once engaged. Speaking about their move toward a less socially conscious approach, Sweeney says that

> . . . by the late nineteenth century, when faced by a whole new world of needy people and social issues, evangelicals retreated from the frontlines of reform. Their fears of social gospel liberalism, combined with the cultural pessimism connected to what is known as a "great reversal" of their posture in society—particularly in its modern, urban settings—one that has haunted evangelicals ever since.[72]

This "reversal," however, must not be overstated, as there were evangelicals who identified with fundamentalists and against the social gospel movement without retreating from social action.[73]

---

69. Olson, *Westminster Handbook*, 37.
70. Ibid.
71. Ibid., 37–38.
72. Sweeney, *American Evangelical*, 163.
73. Ibid., 164.

Evangelicals and Liberation Revisited

## Neoevangelicalism

During the 1930s and 1940s a new group of fundamentalists came into scene attempting to reengage culture while maintaining most of the conservative theological stance of the fundamentalists who preceded them. This different brand of fundamentalists is sometimes called neoevangelicals.[74] These new fundamentalists played an important part in the establishment of institutions such as Fuller Theological Seminary, the Evangelical Theological Society, and the National Association of Evangelicals. The main names connected to this period of the evangelical movement were Carl F. Henry, Harold John Ockenga, Charles E. Fuller, and Billy Graham.

As in the case of every other period in the evangelical movement, one cannot assume that the neoevangelicals were univocal in every issue. If it could be said that there was a somewhat strong consensus among neoevangelicals in the 1930s and 1940s, such a consensus was no longer strong by the 1950s and 1960s. By then, Graham, the most important neoevangelical name of the period, was being opposed publicly by some right-wing fundamentalists, and Fuller Seminary had softened its stance on the doctrine of inerrancy.[75] The 1970s saw a move toward moderation in Lausanne-1974 with its elevation of social action and relativization of inerrancy;[76] however, the Chicago Statement of 1978 with its insistence in considering inerrancy an intrinsic teaching to biblical orthodoxy represents a move that is contrary to the course set by Lausanne-1974.[77] Today, as the great leaders of the neoevangelical approach are passing, scholars speculate if the movement will be able to maintain its coherence.[78] With the increasing evangelical polarization in issues such as inerrancy, homosexuality, postmodernity, God's sovereignty, women in ministry, hermeneutics, narrative theologies, and kenotic Christology,[79] the unity of the evangelical movement as understood by neoevangelicals is threatened. The question raised by Roger Olson is, therefore, of central importance: "Do evangelical theologians

---

74. Ibid., 170.

75. Ibid., 177–78.

76. Warner, *Reinventing English Evangelicalism*, 184–87.

77. Ibid., 196–97.

78. Sweeney, *American Evangelical*, 178.

79. Some of these tensions are mentioned by Roger Olson in "Tensions in Evangelical Theology" in *Dialog: A Journal of Theology* 42/1 (2003): 76.

share sufficient common ground to be considered a relatively united type of contemporary theological reflection?"[80]

## Post-Conservative Evangelical Theology

The diversity within the evangelical movement grew with the rise of what came to be known as Post-Conservative Evangelicalism. Coming into scene in the end of the twentieth century, Post-Conservative Evangelicalism, an approach that will be dealt with in greater detail in chapter 7, reacted against what was perceived as the narrow vision of neoevangelical theology and saw the diversity of Evangelicalism not as a threat but as a condition that is central to the movement. This approach sought to establish a more inclusive understanding of what it means to be evangelical by arguing for a "generous orthodoxy" that could transcend the liberal-conservative spectrum. Two of the main theologians who represent this approach are Roger Olson and Clark Pinnock.

So, given all this diversity and change, who is an evangelical today? For the purpose of this study, David Bebbington's account of the four general characteristics of Evangelicalism and Roger Olson's addition to Bebbington's list will be accepted as the standard for considering any given Christian an evangelical. Bebbington argued that biblicism, conversionism, crucicentrism, and activism in evangelism and social transformation are the core features that identify evangelicals.[81] To this list Olson added "deference to traditional, basic Christian orthodoxy within a higher commitment to the authority of God's Word in Scripture as the norming norm of all Christian faith and practice."[82] In light of the diversity and dynamism within the evangelical movement that the brief overview above attempted to show, this list of five central features is broad enough to do justice to that diversity without loosing its ability as an identifying standard. These features will be revisited in chapter 7, where I will present Post-Conservative Evangelicalism in greater detail.

---

80. Roger Olson, "Tensions in Evangelical," 76.
81. Bebbington, *Evangelicalism in Modern Britain*, 19.
82. Olson, *Reformed and Always Reforming*, 43.

## Conclusion: Evangelicalism and LALT as Theologies of Reaction and Renewal

Due to some of the developments that have been presented above, Evangelicalism and LALT are today closer than they have ever been. On the part of the liberationists, a greater awareness by the stronger, Catholic approach of the necessity to cooperate with Protestants in general and Pentecostals in particular have generated a call for greater ecumenicity and cooperation that, in spite of its different context, resembles the non-partisanship that characterized the early stages of the Great Awakening. Furthermore, developments in the social sciences and economic theory allowed liberationists to be more nuanced regarding their political-economic stance. This is significant for, as we will see in chapter 4, the strong Marxist element that characterized early LALT was heavily criticized, especially by American Evangelicals whose context of aggressiveness toward socialism made any incorporation of it almost immediately unacceptable. With the acceptance of the need to generate wealth by the part of the new generation of LALT and with the American memory of the cold war fading into their historical background, the political-economic aspects of both approaches are hardly incompatible.

The Post-Conservative distancing from the idea held by fundamentalists that rigid doctrinal convictions are the center of Evangelicalism also brought both movements closer together. As I will argue in more detail in chapter 8, the Post-Conservative tendency of valuing transformation over information is, despite its differences in its articulation on the part of LALT, also a central feature of the liberationist movement. As a matter of fact, the Post-Conservative conviction that a centered-set model provides a better description of Evangelicalism than a bounded-set model, though never applied to the liberationist movement, may serve as a model that also better describes LALT itself.

An evident resemblance between the two movements is that both have roots in reactions to a perceived exaggerated focus on orthodoxy that arguably paralyzed other significant aspects of authentic Christian experience. The call for orthopraxis by early liberationists and the insistence on the importance of orthopathy present in the pietistic tendencies of Evangelicalism serve as a reminder that both movements are not only reactionary but are also a challenge to the established churches of their specific context to repent of their reductionisms and incorporate the aspects of authentic Christian living neglected by their approach into their lives and institutions. Granted, these broad historical resemblances are not enough to provide a definitive compatibility between the movements; nevertheless, it is a first step in that direction.

# 3

## Scripture and Hermeneutics

THE ISSUES OF SCRIPTURE and hermeneutics are probably the most controversial ones when it comes to the evangelical-liberationists interaction. Some of this tension is caused by the fact that most of the major liberation theologians were Catholic and consequentially more open to the influence of higher criticism and other hermeneutical tools. In this sense, the evangelical resistance to LALT's use of Scripture and hermeneutics can be, at least in some cases, a reflection of the disagreements between Evangelicalism in general and the RCC. Nevertheless, there are evangelical criticisms that are aimed at particularly liberationist characteristics. As it will be shown below, the liberationist view of Scripture and hermeneutic has been challenged by evangelicals since the first interactions between the two movements. This chapter attempts to do three things:

1. Present the main evangelical criticisms of LALT's approach to Scripture.

2. Present LALT's own articulation of its approach to Scripture and hermeneutics.

3. Show some challenges to the conservative evangelical concept of biblicism.

I hope that this chapter represents, though still mostly implicitly, a move toward my argument for the compatibility of evangelicalism and LALT.

## Evangelical Criticisms of LALT's Use of Scripture and Hermeneutics

Many of the evangelical criticisms of LALT have to do with the issue of contextuality. Because LALT is not concerned with the universality of any given interpretation, it is accused of being partial and reductionistic by evangelical theologians. Evangelical missiologist Harvey Conn argues that though evangelicals can grant that their exegesis is culturally conditioned, the contextuality that LALT calls for cannot do justice to the received tradition of the Gospel. For him, in the LALT approach there is a hermeneutical elevation of history. He contrasts the liberationist approach to the evangelical by saying that "Liberation theology equates hermeneutics to the world, evangelical theology to the Word. To the one, the content of the gospel is defined simply in terms of historical praxis. To the other, it is defined simply in terms of the written Word of God."[1] If the contextualization that LALT argues for is implemented, Conn argues, Scripture will inevitably be historicized from norm to paradigm, from cannon to hermeneutic category.[2] Though Conn is aware that his approach makes him vulnerable to "Bonino's charges of enshrining the truth," he thinks that a proper hermeneutic necessarily runs this risk.[3]

Carl Armerding has a similar criticism to that of Conn. Like Conn, he also acknowledges that pure objectivity is a myth, but he criticizes liberation theology's starting point, which for him is the "culturally or historically conditioned set of circumstances"[4] to which exegesis must adjust. For Armerding, the original context of the text sometimes cuts through the exegete's concept of reality and, consequently, he criticizes LALT for not providing a more universal hermeneutical method.[5]

Evangelical theologian Harold Brown argues that LALT's elevation of historical context to the hermeneutical level is due to its presupposition of the Marxist view of history. For Brown, LALT did not take Scripture or tradition into consideration when developing this presupposition; rather, because of this presupposition, it took as its main source of revelation the consciousness and experience of the oppressed. He condemns this characteristic by

---

1. Conn, "Contextualization," 104.
2. Conn, "The Mission," 82.
3. Conn, "Contextualization," 111.
4. Armerding, "Exodus," 57.
5. Ibid., 57–58.

saying that it is a "Schleiermachian move" once it was liberal theologian Friedrich Schleiermacher who made religious consciousness a source of religious knowledge.[6] Brown goes on to say that by absolutizing the feeling and experience of the oppressed, LALT is absolutizing a non-biblical standard; it is making human feelings a source for divine revelation that can be placed alongside Scripture. According to Brown, to accept any other source of knowledge besides Scripture is inappropriate because to do so is to deny the sovereignty and sufficiency of biblical revelation.[7] Brown is convinced that Christianity is a religion where everything depends on the concept of the Word of God and its interpretation.[8] His rigid position in regards to Scripture and hermeneutics seems to point to a considerably reductionistic view of what Christianity is and who is a true Christian.

One of the most influential evangelical theologians in the United States, Carl F. Henry, sides with the majority of evangelicals in condemning the liberationist approach to Scripture and hermeneutics. For Henry, LALT accepts a Marxist hermeneutic that subverts the biblical revelation. Henry criticizes the socio-political lenses used by liberationists in their interpretation of Scripture; he is convinced that theological reflection must start from biblical revelation.[9] Henry is also convinced that LALT proceeds on the basis of a distorted gospel. and therefore that it serves socialism rather than God. This movement, in Henry's opinion, reflects the shortcomings of a context-controlled hermeneutics at every major doctrinal point. The Bible, then, has only a supporting role in LALT, for scriptural teaching is relativized as contemporary sociological concerns are absolutized. Furthermore, in Henry's opinion, the exegesis of LALT is selective and one-sided, as it does not deal with the whole person and proclaims the "ethic of change" rather than the "ethic of order."[10] For Henry, it is clear that evangelical theology is necessarily at odds with the liberationist approach to Scripture and hermeneutics.

Andrew Kirk, a more moderate critic of the movement, argues that the meaning of the text can be objectively identified with the help of tradition. For him, the Bible can be objectively interpreted if it is not being suppressed and LALT suppresses the Bible by not allowing it to question

---

6. Brown, "What is Liberation," 11.
7. Ibid.
8. Ibid., 5.
9. Henry, "Liberation Theology," 196.
10. Ibid., 200.

its presuppositions.[11] For Kirk, "... it is a basic hermeneutical premise that only by immersing ourselves in the biblical world and being prepared to accept biblical thought-forms shall we ever be able to hear fully the biblical message."[12] Sociological concerns, then, must not guide one's hermeneutic method as in the case of LALT. One cannot help but wonder how Kirk would respond to Gutierrez's statement that

> ... although it is true that we read the Bible, it is also true that the Bible reads us and speaks to us. As the letter to the Hebrews says, the scriptures X-rays us, so to speak. [. . .] Readiness to hear God as God speaks to us in this way is a necessary prerequisite if we are to be open not only to certain texts but to the Bible as a whole.[13]

Statements such as this seem to present evangelical critics with an approach to Scripture and hermeneutics that is closer to their own than they are ready to allow. Despite the fact that liberationists usually emphasize the often-neglected socio-political dimension of hermeneutics, LALT has not necessarily substituted the mystical, personal dimension of Bible reading and interpretation for a purely socio-political approach.

Despite Kirk's criticisms of LALT's hermeneutics, he acknowledges the importance of context. He argues that the greatest possible objectivity is reached when two poles are taken into consideration:

1. The contemporary situation scientifically analyzed.
2. The biblical message interpreted according to its own criteria.[14]

The methodology he proposes is, therefore, an inversion of the method proposed by Gutierrez. Kirk calls for a "...critical reflection on God's Word in the light of a contemporary practice of liberation."[15] Though this seems to be closer to the general liberationist approach, by emphasizing an objective, universal hermeneutic, Kirk also rejects the central claims of the liberationist method.

As seen above, the evangelical criticisms of LALT are usually connected to the issues of Marxism and contextuality. Evangelical theologians who have interacted with LALT seem to acknowledge that context is indeed

---

11. Kirk, *Liberation Theology*, 182–89.
12. Ibid., 192.
13. Gutierrez, *On Job*, xvii–xviii.
14. Kirk, *Liberation theology*, 193.
15. Ibid.

important for interpretation but that it plays no determinative role in regards to the content of the meaning ascribed to the text. The question of how historical context can help in obtaining the objective, trans-locative meaning of the text, however, remains, to my knowledge, unanswered. It seems that passages such as Ephesians 6:5, 1 Corinthians 14:34, or Genesis 1–3 have their meaning determined by the context and particular interests of their interpreters. If that conviction holds true, it is only when there are changes in one's context that are significant to certain interpretative moves that interpreters become aware of the cultural contingency of their own interpretation. Therefore, it is highly unlikely that one hundred years ago the "Bible" would have allowed the election of Rev. Fred Luther—a black man—to the presidency of the Southern Baptist Convention. It is also unlikely that evangelicals would be so concerned with verifiable truth if the Enlightenment had not come.

## The Liberationist Articulation of Its Use of Scripture and Hermeneutics

The approach of LALT to scriptural interpretation can be characterized as a "hermeneutic of suspicion." Liberationists believe, in the words of Juan Luiz Segundo, that "anything and everything involving ideas is intimately bound up with the existing situation in at least an unconscious way."[16] Out of this conviction comes the concern of liberationists with understanding their environment as thoroughly as possible. In order to understand their environment, liberationists make use of the social sciences, particularly Marx's social analysis. However, such an approach is implemented out of a concern for faithfulness to God, a faithfulness which is only authentic if it is manifested in action. This dynamic relationship between social situation and biblical interpretation calls for a hermeneutical circle. Segundo argues that his form of the liberationist hermeneutic circle is characterized by "the continuing change in our interpretation of the Bible which is dictated by the continuing changes in our present day reality."[17]

Segundo's circle develops in four main stages:

1. The experience of reality in an oppressed situation, which leads to ideological suspicion.

---

16. Segundo, *Liberation*, 8.
17. Ibid.

## Scripture and Hermeneutics

2. Application of ideological suspicion to the whole structure of society in general and to theology in particular.
3. A new way of experiencing theology that leads to exegetical suspicion.
4. A new hermeneutic.[18]

Segundo is convinced that theology must change with the questions that come up in response to new concepts of reality. For him, as for other liberation theologians, there is no such thing as simple, eternal, impartial interpretation of Scripture. Segundo argues that when liberationists are accused of partiality they can reply that they are indeed partial, but by being able to acknowledge their partiality they are less prone to the idolatry of their accusers, who by not realizing their own partiality, absolutize the contingent.[19]

Liberationists do not accept the tendency of academic theology to operate as if the influence of contexts affects the theologian—and therefore his or hers biblical interpretation—only marginally. It is exactly this tendency that we see in evangelical criticisms of LALT—the tendency of trying to maintain simultaneously both the importance of context and a trans-locative hermeneutic. For liberation theologians, there can be no interpretation of the gospel message in a vacuum, in the absence of *a priori* commitments.[20] A theologian's response to Scripture is always limited by his or her situation and historical possibilities.[21] The attempts of academic theologians to be "uncontaminated" by secular concepts leaves them ever more vulnerable to the temptation of absolutizing the philosophies that inevitably are smuggled in.[22]

Another characteristic of liberationists thought that has great bearing on their hermeneutics is their conviction that there is no truth outside or beyond "concrete and historical events in which men are involved as agents."[23] According to Bonino, such conviction draws three main criticisms:

1. That biblical truth is reduced to ethical action.
2. That the vertical dimension is swallowed by the horizontal.
3. That this is actually the Marxist concept of knowledge.

18. Ibid., 9.
19. Ibid., 33.
20. Ibid., 94–95.
21. Ibid., 125.
22. Bonino, *Toward*, 45.
23. Bonino, *Doing Theology*, 88.

Bonino answers these objections by showing that Scripture in general and the Old Testament and Johannine literature in particular support such conviction. For him, it is the classical conception of knowledge that is problematic. Bonino argues that

> It seems clear enough that the classical conception can claim no biblical basis for its conceptual understanding of truth or for its distinction between a theoretical knowledge of truth and a practical application of it. Correct knowledge is contingent on right doing. Or, rather, the knowledge is disclosed in the doing.[24]

This conviction points to the fact that the liberationist hermeneutic, with its focus on transformative praxis, is at odds with the general evangelical approach, which focuses on truth as information.

The primacy of praxis in establishing truth means that all biblical interpretation "must be investigated in relation to the praxis out of which it comes."[25] Because a commitment to a given socio-political approach, be it conscious or not, always precedes interpretation, assessing the worth of such commitment is central to the liberationist approach. It is because this socio-political commitment guides interpretation that ideological suspicion is a first step in Segundo's hermeneutical circle. The authenticity of one's interpretation, according to this approach, must be assessed in relation to questions of imperialism, exploitation, racism, sexism, and other socio-political concerns. To do otherwise is to neglect a central feature of the hermeneutical process and to risk giving metaphysical legitimation to constructed truths. Because those who attempt to analyze theology on a "purely conceptual" level ultimately fail to recognize the partiality of every theological stance, their criticisms are not taken seriously by liberationists. In the words of Leonardo and Clodovis Boff,

> ...criticisms made of liberation theology by those who judge it on a purely conceptual level, devoid of any real commitment to the oppressed, must be seen as radically irrelevant. Liberation theology responds to such criticisms with just one question: what part have you played in the effective and integral liberation of the oppressed?[26]

Separating socio-political commitment, praxis, and interpretation is practically impossible in the liberationist approach to hermeneutics.

---

24. Ibid., 90.
25. Ibid., 91.
26. Boff and Boff, *Introducing*, 9.

*Scripture and Hermeneutics*

According to liberationists such as Bonino, because of its insistence on neutrality in establishing the content of the Christian message, the evangelical acknowledgement of the role played by context in the process of interpretation is inadequate. For Bonino, even the most "history-conscious" North-Atlantic theologians fail in their hermeneutical approach. He argues that

> They grant that faith emerges as a historical praxis. Moreover, they grant the political character of this praxis. But then, they want to remain at some neutral or intermediate level in which there is no need to opt for this or that concrete political praxis, i.e., to assume a particular analysis and a particular ideological projection. We have already seen that such an attempt is self-deceptive.[27]

According to liberationists the evangelical attempt of providing a universal hermeneutic is ultimately a denial of the true role played by context in biblical interpretation. This is so because it implies neutrality and unmediated knowledge. As Bonino said:

> We cannot, therefore, take too seriously the frequent warnings and admonitions coming from European and American theologians against our "ideological biases" as if they were speaking from some sort of ideological aseptic environment.[28]

In addition to the liberationist argument that neutrality in interpretation and, consequently, an objective hermeneutic is impossible, evangelical theologians have to deal with the fact that even those who defend the possibility of objectivity in their interpretation of Scripture are, many times, in disagreement when it comes to central doctrinal matters. It is to this matter that this piece now turns.

## The Challenge of Pervasive Interpretive Pluralism

The general evangelical approach to Scripture, which is sometimes referred to as "biblicism," faces serious challenges because of the inconsistency between the exegetical conclusions of those who agree that the Bible can be objectively interpreted. The term "biblicism," of course, can be defined in a number of ways. For the purposes for this chapter, sociologist Christian Smith's definition will be adopted. By "biblicism," Smith means "a theory about the Bible that emphasizes together its exclusive authority, infallibility,

27. Bonino, *Doing Theology*, 95.
28. Ibid., 99.

perspicuity, self-sufficiency, internal consistency, self-evident meaning, and universal applicability."[29] This is a definition that is more specific than the post-conservative definition of "biblicism" that will be mentioned below; however, it is a better one for defining the conservative evangelical approach to the use of Scripture and hermeneutics.

According to Smith, the conservative evangelical biblicism has ten general characteristics. They are:

1. It considers the Bible to be God's own words written in human language in an inerrant way.

2. It sees the Bible as the representation of the totality of God's communication to and will for human kind.

3. It sees the Bible as the divine deposit of God's will about all the issues that Christians will have to deal with during their journey on earth.

4. Conservative evangelical biblicism holds that reasonably intelligent people can understand the Bible's "plain meaning of the text" simply by reading it plainly.

5. Those who ascribe to Smith's notion of biblicism think that the best way to make sense of a biblical text is by reading it in the most obvious, literal sense as it was intended by the author.

6. The importance of any given biblical text can be understood without mediation.

7. The seventh feature of this approach, which Smith calls "Internal Harmony," is the belief that passages of the Bible can be harmonized as if Scripture consisted of "internally consistent bodies of instruction about right and wrong beliefs and behaviors."[30]

8. Conservative evangelical biblicism also argues that the Bible is universally applicable—that is, that what biblical authors taught during their time remains valid unless such teachings are invalidated by subsequent biblical teaching.

9. The belief that all matters of Christian faith and practice are contained in Scripture and, therefore, can be extracted by careful exegesis is Smith's ninth characteristic.

---

29. Smith, *Bible Made*, viii.
30. Ibid., 5.

10. Finally, as a consequence of the nine aforementioned features, Smith argues that conservatives see the Bible as a handbook or textbook for Christian living and that, as such, it teaches Christians how to deal with all manner of subjects including economics, politics, health and science.[31]

Smith argues that conservative evangelical biblicism is rampant among American evangelicals. According to him

> Biblicism can readily be found in the belief statements of scores of denominations, seminaries, and parachurch ministries; seen in the words of myriad Christian authors and speakers; heard in the messages of innumerable pulpits and Bible studies; and observed in the practices of countless personal devotions.[32]

Furthermore, an array of political convictions is given biblical legitimation by conservative evangelicals who approach Scripture in this way. It is not uncommon to hear evangelicals quoting biblical texts as "proof" of their correct stance in regards to issues such as abortion, capital punishment, gay marriage, and even private property.

The issue that Smith identifies in conservative biblicism is what he calls pervasive interpretive pluralism. This problem arises as, according to Smith,

> The very same Bible—which biblicists insist is perspicuous and harmonious—gives rise to divergent understandings among intelligent, sincere, committed readers about what it says about most topics of interest.[33]

This phenomenon brings Smith to the conclusion that

> What that means in consequence is this: in a crucial sense it simply does not matter whether the Bible is everything that biblicists claim theoretically concerning its authority, infallibility, inner consistency, perspicuity, and so on, since in actual functioning the Bible produces a pluralism of interpretations.[34]

Smith argues convincingly that affirming the characteristics of conservative biblicism does not assist in solving the problem of the multiple incompatible readings of the Bible among evangelicals. On the contrary,

31. Ibid., 4–5.
32. Ibid., 6.
33. Ibid., 17.
34. Ibid.

the fact that several contradictory interpretations exist among scholars who affirm characteristics such as inerrancy and perspicuity renders the very affirmation of these characteristics irrelevant.

But one should not think that Smith was the first to notice this problem. He lists a number of respected evangelical academics, church fathers, and reformers who have acknowledged the significance of pervasive interpretive pluralism.[35] After showing the widespread acknowledgement of the issue among evangelicals, in a very direct, conclusive statement, Smith says

> So the question is this: if the Bible is given by a truthful and omnipotent God as an internally consistent and perspicuous text precisely for the purpose of revealing to humans correct beliefs, practices, and morals, then why is it that the presumably sincere Christians to whom it has been given cannot read it and come to common agreement about what it teaches? I know no good answer to that question. If the Bible is all that biblicism claims it to be, then Christians—especially those who share biblicist beliefs—ought to be able to come to a solid consensus about what it teaches, at least on most matters of importance. But they do not and apparently cannot.
>
> Quite the contrary. Christians, perhaps especially biblicist Christians, are "all over the map" on what the Bible teaches about most issues, topics, and questions. In this way, the actual functional outcome of the biblicist view of scripture belies biblicism's theoretical claims about the Bible. Something is wrong in the biblicist picture that cannot be ignored.[36]

The challenges put forth by Smith should not be taken lightly by conservative evangelicals. Why maintain convictions such as inerrancy, perspicuity, or the possibility of a universal hermeneutic if ultimately there is no agreement among them when it comes to the particulars of the faith? And, most importantly, if there is no agreement in the outcome of different conservative evangelical exegeses, what are the factors that guide the different biblical interpretations given by evangelicals who hold to Smith's articulation of biblicism?

It is beyond the scope of this work to answer the questions asked above comprehensively; nevertheless, it is clear that the questions themselves imply that the hermeneutical method of conservative Evangelicalism is fundamentally inadequate. Smith attempts to solve the issue of pervasive interpretative pluralism by appealing to the Roman Catholic Tradition.

35. Ibid., 18–24.
36. Ibid., 26.

Such an attempt, however, fails, as it faces a similar problem: the Roman Catholic Tradition is also interpreted in a plurality of ways by those who claim to be faithful to it. For instance, while Vatican II is celebrated by theologians like Franz Josef Van Beeck, whose main concern is worship, identity, and ecumenicity,[37] liberationists such as Gutierrez want to give priority to the pre-conciliar intentions of John XXIII and the post-conciliar encyclicals of Paul VI because of what they perceive as the shortcomings of the Council regarding its articulation of the causes of poverty and the strategies necessary to eradicate it.[38] While for Van Beeck the openness of the church brought by the Council calls for a greater sense of identity as a body distinct from the world, secularization is emphasized by Gutierrez.

In addition to that, many Roman Catholic theologians since the election of John Paul II have pointed out that both John Paul II and Benedict XVI have resisted the changes tentatively initiated by Vatican II.[39] According to some Roman Catholic critics, the conservatism of both Wojtyla and Ratzinger led them to reject any significant attempt toward *aggiornamento* made by those who wanted to further implement the changes initiated by the Council. These examples seem to discredit Smith's suggestion of appealing to the Roman Catholic Tradition as a way of solving the issue of pervasive interpretive pluralism. Because the tradition of the RCC is also interpreted in a variety of ways and such interpretations are often found to be conveniently selective, the same criticism made by Smith of conservative

---

37. See Frans Jozef van Beeck, *God Encountered: A Contemporary Systematic Theology*, Vol. 1 (Collegeville: Michael Glazier, 1989): 3, 71, 92, and 162–63; and Frans Jozef van Beeck, *Catholic Identity after Vatican II: Three Types of Faith in One Church* (Chicago: Loyola University Press, 1983): 1, 2, 4, 23, and 48.

38. For examples of Gutierrez's prioritization of John XXIII's pre-conciliar intentions and Paul VI's encyclicals as well as his criticisms of Vatican II see Gustavo Gutierrez, *We Drink from Our Own Wells: The Spiritual Journey of a People*, trans. by Matthew J. O'Connell (Maryknoll: Orbis Books, 1983): 29; Gustavo Gutierrez, *The God of Life* trans. by Matthew J. O'Connell (Maryknoll: Orbis Books, 1991): 188; Gustavo Gutierrez, "The Church and the Poor: A Latin American Perspective" in *The Reception of Vatican II* edited by Giuseppe Alberigo et all (Washington: The Catholic University of America Press, 1987): 171–72, 180, and 184; and Gustavo Gutierrez, *A Theology of Liberation: History, Politics, and Salvation*, trans. by Sister Caridad and John Eagleson (Maryknoll: Orbis Books, 1988): xxi, xxvi, 7, 22–25, 30, 38, 98–99, and 162–65.

39. See *The Church in Anguish: Has the Vatican Betrayed Vatican II?* Edited by Hand Kung and Leonard Swindler (San Francisco: Harper & Row, 1987); and *Vatican II: A Forgotten Future?* edited by Alberto Melloni and Christoph Theobald (London: SCM Press, 2005).

evangelical hermeneutics can be made, at least to some extent, of interpreters of the Roman Catholic Tradition.

It seems, therefore, that factors that are external to the perceived sources of revelation (e.g. Bible and tradition) such as context and personal experience have a bigger role in the hermeneutical process than conservative evangelicals are willing to acknowledge. If context is indeed determinative of one's interpretation of Scripture, the liberationist approach to Scripture and hermeneutics offers a plausible explanation for the issue of pervasive interpretative pluralism in both conservative evangelical and Roman Catholic circles. This means that any distancing of liberationists from biblicism is warranted, insofar as by "biblicism" one means the conservative approach to biblicism which includes the doctrines of inerrancy, perspicuity, and the possibility of a metaphysically legitimized hermeneutic. There is no contradiction, however, as it will be argued below, between the liberationist approach to Scripture and lighter articulations of biblicism which focus on one's disposition toward the Bible.

# 4

# Marxism, Socialism, and Violence

A CENTRAL FOCUS OF the criticisms that conservative North Atlantic Evangelicals make of Latin American Liberation Theology is the liberationist dialogue with Marxism, its commitment to striving for a socialist society, and LALT's endorsement of violence. Although it is not necessary to ascribe Marxism and violence to LALT,[1] the majority of Latin American liberationists do include, to various degrees, the three above mentioned elements into their theology. The diversity of evangelical responses to these issues must also be acknowledged. However, it is not the intent of this piece to be exhaustive regarding the diversity of evangelical responses, but to present the conservative evangelical responses to these issues—the responses that are primarily based on conservative-evangelical reactions to the ideas developed in the foundational stages of LALT and that still have a significant force in influencing contemporary perceptions of LALT on the part of NAEvs.

This chapter will be divided in two parts. First, I will present evangelical criticisms of LALT in connection with Marxism, Socialism, and violence. Again, these criticisms do not exhaust the spectrum within Evangelicalism, but are representative of the approach of the most conservative

1. Hugo Assmann's and Jung Mo Sung's acknowledgement of Jose Comblin's criticism of Marxism and other forms of hegelianisms in the 1960s shows that not all liberationists borrow heavily from Marx (see Hugo Assmann and Jung Mo Sung. *Deus em Nós: O Reinado que Acontece no Amor Solidario aos Pobres*. [São Paulo: Paulus, 2010]: 111). Furthermore, it is widely known that major liberationists such as Leonardo Boff and Dom Helder Câmara were already pacifists during the foundational period of the movement (see Leonardo Boff. *Jesus Christ Liberator: A Critical Christology for Our Times*. [Maryknoll: Orbis Books, 1978] and Jose Miguez-Bonino. *Doing Theology in a Revolutionary Situation*. [Philadelphia: Fortress Press, 1975]).

sects of the movement and thus highly influential in the popular expression of the same. Secondly, I will present the general liberationist articulation of its use of Marx, an example of the liberationist approach to the Capitalism-Socialism tension of "new-generation" liberationist Jung Mo Sung, and a brief discussion of the apparent inconsistency among evangelicals who criticize LALT's endorsement of violence while endorsing violence themselves.

## Marxism, Socialism, and Violence: The Evangelical Criticism

### Criticism of the Use of Marxist Tools

NAEvs in general praise the goals of LALT while condemning what they perceive as its central characteristics. Three of these characteristics that are strongly opposed by NAEvs are Marxism, Socialism, and LALT's endorsement of violence. Writing in the 90s Belli and Nash argue that the early LALT should repent of the harm which their bad social theory and economics have done to the poor in the south.[2] Although they acknowledge a shift within LALT as it becomes, in their opinion, more democratic, more orthodox, less Marxist, more responsible with Scripture, and more concerned with spirituality,[3] they argue that its allegiance to Marxism is still too strong and consequently inappropriate.[4] For Belli and Nash, using Marxist tools (e.g. social analysis) is tantamount to using Marxist ideology and strategies; according to them, LALT, especially in its early stages, is guilty of being full fledge Marxist as long as it insists in using any Marxist tool.[5]

Another criticism of LALT's use of Marx is its relationship with Marx's philosophy of history.[6] By deeming both Marx's social analysis and his philosophy of history inappropriate, evangelical critics argue for LALT's inability to read the "signs of time" properly in their continent. Because tools such as Marx's social analysis are widely used by LALT in its attempt to contextualize theology so that it can be relevant in the Latin America situation, considering it inappropriate may generate a negative reaction to the whole of LALT. The limited scope and usefulness of tools such as Marxism are recognized by Latin American liberationists; however, LALT in general

---

2. Belli and Nash, *Beyond Liberation*, 29.
3. Ibid., 23–24.
4. Ibid., 55–57.
5. Ibid., 67–71.
6. Brown, "What is Liberation," 7.

is still characterized by the influence of Marxist thinking on its theological, political, and economic articulations. Therefore, the conservative evangelical attack on Marxism is significant, as it challenges the foundational presuppositions of LALT.

## Criticism of LALT's Socialism

Conservative evangelicals also respond negatively to the liberationist conviction that some form of socialism must be implemented. Capitalism is the economic system of choice for NAEvs in general, and socialism is consequentially seen in a negative light. Theologian Ronald Nash, an influential thinker among conservative evangelical circles, was an avid defender of Free Market Capitalism (henceforth FMC). His position is a trustworthy representation of the position held by conservative evangelicals who have carefully thought about harmonizing their capitalist convictions with Christianity. For Nash, LALT has three foundational claims:

1. That Christians must be politically active on behalf of the oppressed.
2. That the major cause of poverty and oppression in Latin America is capitalism.
3. That socialism should replace capitalism.

He agrees with the first claim but rejects the other two.[7] Though both liberationists and conservative evangelicals can affirm with Barth that "faith that believes in God the father, the son, and the Holy Spirit cannot refuse to become public,"[8] they articulate their public responsibility and allegiances in considerably different ways.

According to Nash, FMC is the best way to eradicate poverty.[9] Nash argues that true capitalism is a peaceful means of exchange based on voluntary relationships. To counter capitalism, in his opinion, is to go against the only system which effectively fights injustice.[10] The efforts of what he calls economic interventionism, which advocates for state intervention in the economy in order to attain certain social goals, undermine the best interest

---

7. Nash, "The Christian Choice," 49.
8. Barth, *Dogmatics*, 29.
9. Nash, "The Christian Choice," 49.
10. Ibid, 54.

of society as a whole.[11] Therefore, if some of the American economic practices deserve condemnation, it is economic interventionism that must be criticized. This means that, for Nash, when liberationists condemn the immoral economic practices of first world nations and name those practices "capitalism," they are making a fundamental mistake; what they are really describing is interventionism.[12]

Nash argues that capitalism is not only morally superior to any other system but that it is the system most compatible with Christianity.[13] The moral superiority of capitalism is manifested in four main characteristics:

1. Its stress upon voluntary exchanges and transformation helps to encourage respect for other human beings.

2. Private ownership can be a major stimulus to the development of moral behavior.

3. Its emphasis on the sanctity of contract also carries with it important moral expectations.

4. Capitalism provides moral training and character elevation by the fact that nothing is free.[14] For him, the reason why capitalism did not find absolute expression in history and create a just society is humanity's sinful nature.[15]

Capitalism needs Christianity, he argues, not as something which will tame it, but as something that can allow the principles of capitalism to flourish. According to Nash, capitalists who are immoral are enemies of the system.

In *Beyond Liberation Theology* Belli and Nash criticize LALT's social analysis for being reductionistic, for not providing empirical verification of its assumptions, and for its simplistic tendencies to prescribe socialism as a redemptive or liberating sociopolitical system.[16] Furthermore, they assert that LALT fails to account for a central issue helping to keep Latin Americans in poverty—namely, its culture. Belli and Nash argue that Latin Americans have a culture of low productivity, lack of responsibility, poor compliance with standards, and lack of punctuality. For them, it is the

11. Ibid, 58.
12. Ibid., 51.
13. Ibid, 60–65.
14. Ibid., 60–61.
15. Ibid, 55.
16. Belli and Nash, *Beyond Liberation*, 135–39.

defective work ethic and moral patterns of Latin Americans that must be blamed for the continent's underdevelopment.[17] In addition, Belli and Nash trace the cultural heritage of Latin America to the Spaniards, who they consider to be less religiously oriented and therefore less moral than the Anglos who came to the United States. For them, the solution for economic stagnation is capitalism paired with a new religious-Christian morality.[18] Belli's and Nash's articulation is neither the exception nor an anomaly in the West.[19]

## An Alternative Explanation for the Failure of Capitalism in Latin America

Explaining the failure of capitalism in Latin America, however, can take different forms than those defended by Belli and Nash. Peruvian economist Hernando de Soto is one example of a free market capitalist who has provided alternative answers to the issue of the failed implementation of capitalism in Latin America. Reacting to those who, like Belli and Nash, argue for a cultural answer to the issue, Soto says that according to such views

> If (Latin America) failed to prosper despite all the excellent advice, it is because something is the matter with them: they missed the protestant reformation, or they are crippled by the disabling legacy of colonial Europe, or their IQs are too low.[20]

However, in his opinion

> ... the suggestion that it is culture that explains the success of diverse places such as Japan, Switzerland, and California, and culture again explains the relative poverty of such equally diverse places as China, Estonia, and Baja California, is worse than inhumane, is unconvincing.[21]

---

17. Ibid., 152–58.
18. Ibid., 166–70.
19. Catholic theologian Michael Novak is another highly influential thinker who has similar opinions to those of Belli and Nash regarding capitalism and LALT. For a classic expression of Novak's arguments see Michael Novak, *The Spirit of Democratic Capitalism* (Bolder: Madison Books, 1990).
20. Soto, *The Mystery of Capital*, 4.
21. Ibid.

In Soto's view, what is lacking in Latin American countries is a representational process which connects assets to the rest of the economy so that such assets can have "parallel life alongside their material existence."[22] For him,

> It is the unavailability of these essential representations that explains why people who have adopted every other Western invention, from the paper clip to the nuclear reactor, have not been able to produce sufficient capital to make their domestic capitalism work.[23]

The reason why such system has not been efficiently exported, says Soto, is that Westerners take for granted the very mechanisms that make up this system, causing them to lose all awareness of their existence. This system is a legal infrastructure hidden within the Western property system of which ownership is only the tip of the iceberg.[24] If capitalism is to prosper in Latin America, argues Soto, such a system must be clearly articulated and implemented in the continent.

Beyond Soto's contribution of providing an alternative answer to the argument that the culture of Latin America is somehow inferior to that of Western countries—an answer that will not have its reliability analyzed since such effort goes beyond the scope of this work—Soto also provides insight into the conflictive reality of the continent. Soto contends that

> Outside the West advocates of capitalism are intellectually on the retreat. Ascendant just a decade ago, they are now increasingly viewed as apologists for the miseries and injustices that still affect the majority of the people.[25]

According to Soto, because conservative legal establishments that are uninterested in change were given the responsibility of administering the economy of Latin American countries in general, "advocates of globalization and free market reforms are beginning to be perceived as the self-satisfied defenders of the interests of those who dominate the bell jar."[26] In this reality, because the majority is not given access to significantly participate in the market, class confrontation is a real possibility. Soto, a respected capitalist, argues that one should not celebrate the victory of Neoliberalism too soon; the concept of class confrontation did not die with the fall of

22. Ibid., 6.
23. Ibid., 7.
24. Ibid., 8.
25. Ibid., 209.
26. Ibid., 211–12.

the Berlin wall. He argues that it is hard for citizens of advanced countries to understand this because, in Western countries, there are only "pockets of poverty." The poverty in developing and former communist countries, however, cannot be contained in pockets; in these places the pockets are "pockets of wealth."[27]

Hernando de Soto's work shows that even among free market capitalists, there is no consensus regarding the reason for the perceived failure of capitalism in Latin America—or for the reality of social tension in the continent. His acceptance of the conflictive reality of Latin America, where the major part of the population lives in some kind of tension with the "pockets of wealth," is consistent with the Marxist-inspired, liberationist view of reality as conflictive. Soto's example also puts the conviction of the inevitable victory of Neoliberalism in check—a conviction advertised by capitalists since the fall of the Berlin Wall. The ascendancy of former Catholic Bishop and liberationist Fernando Lugo to the presidency of Paraguay (who, according to Leonardo Boff, fully identifies with liberation theology and plans to implement it in his government); and the recent democratic election of Francois Hollande (the first French socialist president since the fall of the Wall) add significant weight to the argument that Neoliberalism claimed its victory prematurely.

## Criticism of LALT's Endorsement of Violence

The endorsement of violence by LALT is criticized by evangelicals of many persuasions. Pacifists are somewhat consistent in their criticism, as they criticize violence regardless of its origin and therefore are, for the most part, not nationalistic in their assessment of the use of violence.[28] However, pacifists can be criticized for their general inability to convincingly articulate a concept of non-violence that accounts for "objective violence" in either its symbolic or systemic forms; that is, their inconsistency lies in ignoring the fact that the "non-violent" background against which subjective violence is experienced and measured is set up and maintained by objective violence

---

27. Ibid., 212.

28. For examples see Ronald J. Sider, *Non-Violence: The Invincible Weapon?* (Dallas: Word Publishing, 1989) and Stanley Hauerwas, *War and the American Difference: Theological Reflections on Violence and National Identity* (Grand Rapids: Baker Academic, 2011). Though Hauerwas may not call himself evangelical, his influence among evangelicals is undeniable.

itself.[29] Though the limited account of non-violence by pacifists is worth mentioning, a bigger inconsistency haunts non-pacifist evangelicals who criticize the general approach toward violence endorsed by LALT.

There are different ways of resisting the notion of revolutionary violence endorsed by LALT. Two common ways are:

1. To emphasize the value of suffering for the Christian life.
2. To claim that "just war" can only be done in submission to the state.

As it will be argued in greater detail below, both options, according to LALT, support the ideology of the status quo. Furthermore, I will attempt to show that both approaches are inappropriate, for while the former is in imminent danger of sacramentalizing suffering, the latter is reductionistic in its articulation of the just war theory it claims to adopt.

Dayton Roberts, in an article entitled *Where Has Liberation Theology Gone Wrong?*, provides an example of the first way of resisting LALT's endorsement of violence. This piece was published by America's main evangelical magazine, namely, *Christianity Today*. For Roberts, LALT errs in neglecting what he thinks is central to authentic Christianity: "The positive place of suffering, martyrdom, and the 'cross' in Christian experience."[30] In his opinion, "Oppression and tyranny—like sickness and suffering—may be a part of God's disciplinary plan for His people."[31] Although Roberts's affirmation may be considered theologically sound, the social consequences of such conviction cannot be overlooked. Conformism and determinism, features that seem to result from Roberts's theological approach, have played into the hands of social conservatives in general and into the hands of the powerful in Latin America in particular.

Raymond Hundley argues for the second response. He thinks that the concept of "just war" cannot evolve into a concept of "just revolution."[32] For him, the "biblical position" does not warrant armed revolt against the state.[33] Consequently, violence is warranted as long as it is justified by some form of just war theory and exercised by the state. This highlights two characteristics of evangelicals who hold similar positions: first, they condemn any kind of armed violence directed toward the established order; secondly, they give the

29. Zizec, *Violence*, 1–4.
30. Roberts, "Where Has Liberation," 1400.
31. Ibid.
32. Hundley, *Radical Liberation*, 48.
33. Ibid.

status of competent authority solely to the state. The potential problems of this approach will be analyzed in light of just war theory and LALT below.

## Marxism, Socialism, and Violence: A Liberationist Account

### The Use of Marx in LALT

The fact that LALT has evolved since its foundation in the 60s is widely recognized. Nevertheless, it must be stated that the relationship between LALT and Marxism never was one of blind acceptance of the latter by the former; *au contraire*, liberationists in general were critical of Marxism from the very beginning while, at the same time, not shying away from using analytic tools developed by Marx. This fact is so widely accepted outside evangelical circles that even Antonio Lopez Trujillo, the conservative cardinal appointed by the Vatican to diminish the influence of the movement in Latin America, openly recognized that LALT itself is not Marxist.[34]

In addition to that, several shifts in LALT that have to do with its position in regard to Marxism have taken place since the 80s. Paul Sigmund points out four such shifts:

1. The shift from infatuation with social revolution to a recognition that the poor will not be liberated by a cataclysmic event of political transformation.

2. The shift from a strong acceptance of Marxist social analysis and dependency theory to a more nuanced attitude toward Marxism and the social sciences.

3. The shift from antagonism toward developmentalism to acceptance of balance and accommodation.

4. The shift in emphasis from the political process to spirituality.

Despite these shifts, it is important to notice that LALT kept its structural anti-capitalism, its drive toward the implementation of socialist policies, its grass-roots populism, and its suspicion of the liberal tradition in politics and philosophy.[35]

The shifts in LALT, however, should not surprise those who are aware of the fact that every theology—and especially theologies that claim to be

---

34. Sigmund, *Liberation Theology*, 93.
35. Ibid., 177–82.

contextual—undergoes revisions due to changes in the environment in which it is developed. The changes within LALT, therefore, do not serve as proof of its inappropriateness, but as evidence of its dynamic engagement with its context. Gutierrez's acknowledgement of the obsolete nature of some of his past assumptions regarding the social sciences provides an example of such dynamic engagement. Speaking about the use of tools for social analysis in the introduction to the second edition of *A Theology of Liberation*, he says that

> The tools used in this analysis vary according to their proven effectiveness for gaining knowledge of social reality and finding solutions for social problems. Science is by its nature critical of its own presuppositions and achievements; it moves on to new interpretive hypotheses. It is clear, for example, that the theory of dependence, which was so extensively used in the early years of our encounter with the Latin American world, is now an inadequate tool, because it does not take sufficient account of the internal dynamics of each country or of the vast dimensions of the world of the poor. In addition, Latin American social scientists are increasingly alert to factors of which they were not conscious earlier and which show the world economy has evolved.[36]

Marxism is one such tool that was overly trusted in the past but is now appropriated more carefully.

Leonardo and Clodovis Boff also nuance their endorsement of Marxist tools. According to them, LALT "maintains a decidedly critical stance in relation to Marxism. Marx can be a companion on the way, but he can never be the guide because you can only have one teacher, the Christ."[37] Porfirio Miranda, who once found clear parallels between Marx and the Bible, criticized Marxism as reductionistic by the end of his career.[38] Marxist tools are used by LALT as tools for reading reality, and even as such their limitations are now widely recognized. As Ribeiro suggests, if up to the 1980s there was an idolatrous inclination in LALT's identification of the Christian faith with the social and ethical conquests of the period's socialism, in the second half of the decade there was a distancing and a more realist criticism of "real socialism."[39]

36. Gutierrez, *A Theology of Liberation*, xxiv.
37. Boff and Boff, *Introducing*, 28.
38. McGovern, *Liberation*, 146.
39. Ribeiro, *A Teologia*, 63.

The use of Marxist tools by LALT was, for the most part, limited to the collecting of data for the process of theologizing. Though liberationists regard theology and the social sciences to be constitutive of each other, the function of the latter is only determinative insofar as it provides the data on which theology is built.[40] This is true of LALT throughout its existence. The fact that Marxism is not as much relied upon as before means that LALT is using recently developed tools for analyzing reality, rather than that it is less interdisciplinary. Interdisciplinarity as a methodological value allows theology to articulate biblical content with a scientific comprehension of reality while, at the same time, letting it criticize the absolutisms of "scientific truth."[41] Though it can be argued that the absolutization of a particular interpretation of reality is a constant danger for the liberationist position, irrelevance is, in the liberationist mind, a bigger danger.

## Jung Mo Sung: An Alternative Liberationist Socialism

Because of the new reality brought by the widespread influence of economic neoliberalism, some liberationists have articulated their stance toward the new global context afresh. Jung Mo Sung is one of such theologians. This Korean-Brazilian Catholic thinker is heavily influenced by Franz Hinkelammert's and Hugo Assmann's critique of the neoliberal agenda. A professor at the Methodist University of São Paulo, Sung is not only ecumenical but also nuanced in his embrace of Marxism, as he recognizes the necessity of a market. However, as it will be seen below, Sung does not hold back in his criticism of neoliberalism in general and FMC in particular. Central to his theological agenda is the "unmasking" of neoliberalism and the argument for the necessity of what he calls "ethical indignation" in any authentic Christian expression. Below, I will present aspects of Sung's criticism of neoliberalism, his concept of ethical indignation, and his general approach to the idea of a market. This will be done as an attempt to present the reader with an articulation of these issues by a "new generation" liberationist and consequently to show that while LALT continues to be anti-capitalist, its articulation of socio-political strategies has moved significantly closer to that of North Atlantic Evangelicalism since the 60s.

The term "neoliberalism" was coined during the late 90s to describe the social and moral effects of the free trade policies of the post-Soviet globalized

40. Phan, "Method," 44–45.
41. Ribeiro, *A Teologia*, 77.

economy. The key institutions of neoliberalism are the IMF and the World Bank, whose impositions make the economies of developing countries increasingly dependent.[42] According to Sung, the fundamental ideas of neoliberalism have their most classic and influential articulation in the ideas of Adam Smith. Smith analyzes economic phenomena as manifestations of a natural order which, in order to operate efficiently, must work with the greatest amount of freedom possible.[43] The state, then, must relinquish its position as coordinator of the social division of labor and give it to the market, which is then overseen by a state whose solely objective is protecting its liberty (i.e., laissez faire). For Sung though, when that happens the state embraces a fictitious representative character where the interests of the majority of the electorate are at best secondary.[44] Since in this approach the market is the driving force of the world, those who are incapable of consuming and producing do not participate in its logic and end up being excluded. This situation is aggravated when corporations acquire a high amount of freedom. Because their motivation is diminishing costs in order to increase profit, corporate interests conflict with social objectives and social inclusion.[45]

Nash's arguments, as seen above, clearly show what neoliberalism claims to accomplish. First, it claims to be a system that can realize *historically* what Christianity transcendentalizes—namely, the manifestation of a completely just society. As long as humans do not fall into the temptation of doing good,[46] the market will freely solve society's problems. Sung notices that in this approach there is an inversion of the love commandment; to love is not to be in solidarity with the Other, but to protect one's own interests in the market.[47] Furthermore, such an absolute claim shows that FMC, as in the case of Marxist socialism, is characterized by the idolatrous pretension of accomplishing the humanly impossible. FMC de-eschatologizes reality so that the possibility of a coming system is inexistent.[48] Here we see Sung's negativity toward FMC but also his suspicion of Marxism, as he criticizes

---

42. de la Torre, *Doing Ethics*, 78–81.
43. Sung, *Teologia*, 176.
44. Miguez et al., *Beyond the Spirit*, 20.
45. Ribeiro, *A Teologia*, 9–11.
46. For an articulation by a major capitalist thinker regarding the supposedly negative effects of interventions with positive social objectives see Friedrich Hayek, *Individualism and Economic Order* (Chicago: The University of Chicago Press, 1948).
47. Sung, *Desire, Market, and Religion*, 16.
48. Miguez et al., *Beyond the Spirit*, 21.

what he sees as the idolatrous tendency of both systems. For Sung, the ideal system is still a system-to-come. He is convinced that such a system is some sort of democratic socialism, but he does not attempt to articulate the features of such a system with a significant degree of specificity.

Sung claims that capitalism cannot exist alongside forms of social organization which place certain values above the logic of the market and of the criterion of technical efficiency.[49] Because, according to capitalists like Nash, to intervene in the market's freedom is sin; the efficacy of the market system becomes the supreme moral standard.[50] Nash, Novak, and other free market capitalists fail to acknowledge that while human sin will not be eliminated in history, it is possible to search for ways to structurally limit its consequences. In addition to that, the FMC system uses the concept of "necessary" sacrifices as a central idea for the articulation of the process of self-regulation. In other words, before society is freed from its problems, the sacrifice of the weak and unproductive is necessary. Therefore, FMC provides a false theology of retribution, where injustices are sacralized and the victims are blamed for their victimization.[51] Even though FMC does not use religious concepts, it provides a theology with the promise of paradise, the explanation of the fundamental cause of suffering, and the necessary prices for salvation.[52] For Sung, this theology is an idolatrous, false theology that should be dismissed by Christians.

Sung argues that implicit in the Neoliberal endeavor are consequences which, as mentioned above, go beyond the economic realm. In the capitalist worldview, where the fundamental objective is to accumulate capital, commodities not only have value but also meaning.[53] As a matter of fact, the primary social function of things is no longer satisfying the desire of consumers but conveying meaning.[54] As a result of this phenomenon, quality of life is equated with quantity of consumption. Moreover, the subjectivity produced by the elite has a significant role in the formation of the Other's subjectivity, a phenomenon known as "mimetic desire."[55] The economic implications of such desire are disastrous for poor nations. The wealthy

49. Sung, *Teologia*, 217.
50. Ibid,. 179.
51. Sung, *Desire, Market, and Religion*, 73.
52. Ibid,. 12.
53. Sung, *Se Deus Existe*, 51.
54. Sung, *Sujeito e Sociedades*, 9.
55. Miguez et al., *Beyond the Spirit*, 37.

of such nations need to appropriate more wealth and concentrate more income in their hands in order to have access to the commodities of the world's elite.[56] At the existential level, economic neoliberalism transforms the relationship between people into a relationship between things; this is why the relationship between people is becoming increasingly ruled by the commodities that they produce and/or consume. In the words of Paul Tillich, ultimate concern with success, social standing, and economic power

> . . . is the God of many people in the highly competitive Western culture and it does what every ultimate concern must do: it demands unconditional surrender to its laws even if the price is the sacrifice of genuine human relations, personal convictions, and creative eros.[57]

The strength of this characteristic has persuaded few scholars to argue that the only subject of the FMC system is the market itself.[58]

Even though the economic and social situation of many around the world is worsened by neoliberalism, Christians refuse to act against it. This happens because such system is socially and religiously legitimized. Cuban-American ethicist Miguel de la Torre argues that this legitimation can be seen in the contributions of three of the most influential Christian ethicists of the twentieth century: namely, Walter Rauschenbusch, Reinhold Niebuhr, and Stanley Hauerwas. Though space constraints make it impossible to deal with these three important Christian ethicists extensively, it is important to identify their contributions to the process of the legitimation of the logic of Empire that is also present in neoliberalism.

De la Torre argues that Walter Rauschenbusch must be commended for his advocacy in favor of the poor. The shortcomings of his ethical system are manifested in his opinions regarding the cultural superiority of the "Teutonic" race and in his support of the US's colonization efforts, which is made explicit in his support of the Spanish-American war.[59] Furthermore, Rauschenbusch wanted black Americans to act like the Euro-American man and to adopt white middle-class values. Therefore, Rauschenbusch argues for the end of what he saw as an oppressive capitalism in the US while at the same time endorsing both racial superiority and colonialism.[60] He

---

56. Ibid., 38.

57. Tillich, *Dynamics of Faith*, 3.

58. Miguez et al., *Beyond the Spirit*, 37–38.

59. de la Torre, *Latina/o Ethics*, 8–10.

60. For both Rauschenbusch's preferential option for the poor and his racial prejudices see Walter Rauschenbusch, *Christianizing the Social Order* (New York: The Macmillan

did not see Western imperialism as a problem per se, but only the attitude of Christians within it.⁶¹

Reinhold Niebuhr's ethical position came to be known as Christian realism. Despite the convenient name, De la Torre thinks that his system lacks the multiplicity of perspectives and multiple consciousnesses necessary for any reliable perception of reality. According to De la Torre, Niebuhr fails to realize that his definition of reality serves the purpose of those who wish to maintain the status quo. Niebuhr follows Augustine in his placing of order over justice, and he ends up developing an ethical paradigm which gives a "preferential option for the political and economic interests of the US."⁶² De la Torre points out that though Niebuhr's early writings show a great amount of identification with issues of social justice due to his experience among the poor of Detroit, his later writings support the US's role as world leader over and against communism.⁶³ Because in Niebuhr's system order was always given precedence over justice, the issue for him was never which system should be put in place to achieve the greatest possible amount of justice; rather, his concern was with the implementation of the greatest amount of justice possible within the established order. Therefore, as Jose Miguez Bonino observes, Niebuhr tolerates the injustices of the elite, and his pragmatism plays into the hand of the status quo.⁶⁴

De la Torre also criticizes the ethical stance of Stanley Hauerwas. Although Hauerwas does not necessarily legitimize the neoliberal mission, he seems to overlook the necessity of urgently acting against it. For him, ethics is orthodoxy. He says that "the first task of Christian social ethics, therefore, is not to make the world better or more just, but to help Christian people to form their community consistent with their conviction that the story of Christ is a truthful account of our existence."⁶⁵ By saying this Hauerwas not only betrays his apathy toward establishing a justice-based society, but he also privileges Eurocentric interpretations of the Christian narrative by confusing what the Bible says with what he interprets it to say. De la Torre argues

Company, 1915). For arguments regarding Rauschenbusch's nationalism, elitism, and racism see Miguel de la Torre, *Latina/o Ethics* (Waco: Baylor University Press, 2010): 7–10 and Warren L. Vinz, *Pulpit Politics: Faces of American Protestant Nationalism in the Twentieth Century* (New York: State University of New York Press, 1997): 95–97.

61. de la Torre, *Latina/o Ethics*, 12–13.
62. Ibid., 14–20.
63. Ibid.
64. Bonino, *Toward*, 87–89.
65. Cited by Miguel de la Torre in *Latina/o Ethics*, 22.

that behind Hauerwas's hermeneutics is a commitment to a preferential option for a church, which is, beyond its criticism of the system, politically uninvolved.[66] Therefore, Hauerwas's ethics acknowledges the importance of justice but fails to make it a fundamental requirement for society.

Sung's and De la Torre's arguments attempt to show the dangers of neoliberalism and how Western society has harmonized it with Christian convictions by using different ethical paradigms that give neoliberalism the freedom to disseminate its doctrine. Many times NAEvs assimilate the precepts of neoliberalism without giving proper consideration to its presuppositions, ideas, and consequences. Nobody does evil in the name of evil itself; neoliberalism is no exception. But, as Sung points out, because our actions present us with a number of possible effects, the structures that mediate our actions and their effects must be understood.[67] Good intentions are not enough for the construction of a more just society. Greater control of the unintentional effects of our actions and the awareness that moral questioning presupposes a conflict between immediate and long-term interests, as well as between private and collective interests is necessary.[68] In order for Christians to prioritize long-term and collective goals, Sung suggests embracing what he calls "ethical indignation." According to him, ethical indignation is the experience which allows people to unmask evil disguised as normality.[69] He argues that it primarily involves two things:

1. The recognition of the other person as human, which may be difficult in a culture where one's humanity is being confused with one's social status.
2. The appreciation of a utopian horizon of an environment where persons are respected and acknowledged independently of their social status.[70]

Ethical indignation reminds Christians that it is impossible to profess faith in the God revealed by Jesus Christ while living a life which shows insensibility toward the situation of the marginalized. Those who have it, be they Christians or not, are the ones capable of hearing the cries of the oppressed; theirs is the job of "negating the pretense divinity of the free market system and of searching for alternatives that can make possible the reality of

66. de la Torre, *Latina/o Ethics*, 23.
67. Sung, *Conversando*, 18–19.
68. Ibid., 22.
69. Sung, *Conversando*, 17.
70. Sung, "The Human Being," 5.

## Marxism, Socialism, and Violence

a dignified life for all."[71] The unmasking of neoliberalism shows that the most basic political decisions, which are presented as invisible laws, can have disastrous consequences. Ethical indignation embraces the responsibility that comes with the awareness of the political effects of our acts.[72]

Though Sung heavily criticizes the absolutization of the market, he sees value in some sort of market. In *Deus em Nós*, a book that Sung co-authored with the once radical theologian Hugo Assmann, a significant shift in the liberationist approach to the market is obvious. According to Sung and Assmann, "The sectarian left was a religious being of the fundamentalist kind and of narrow beliefs. [. . .] It took almost twenty years for the traditional left to start noticing that, in ample and complex societies, the market is an indispensable mechanism for an active and constructive economy."[73] Criticizing the convictions of the founding theologians of LALT (and Assmann is one such founding theologian) regarding their bias against any development that comes from outside of their concept of rupture with the market system, to Assmann and Sung ". . .it seems that, for [the founding theologians of LALT], political rupture is more important than the inclusion of the poor because of their conviction that inclusion without rupture would be a betrayal of the real cause, which for them is the liberation from capitalism."[74]

Assman and Sung go as far as arguing for positive uses of assistencialism, an unlikely position for liberationists of the first generation (and Assmann is a first-generation liberationist). As seen above, Assmann and Sung assume a critical position toward the idea that only attitudes of rupture with the market system can be positive and beneficial for the poor. They do not agree with the argument that the poor who are helped by actions of a reformist nature are excluded from the discourse of the left—the discourse that dictates what is good and what is not good for the poor from the category of rupture-revolution-liberation.[75] The positivity of some forms of assistencialism is defended by Assmann and Sung because, according to them, when such assistance is seen not as an end in itself but as part of the work of conscientization, its long and medium-term results will favor the liberationist cause.[76] For them, even assistencialism, when practiced

---

71. Sung, *Se Deus Existe*, 65.
72. Bonino, *Toward*, 12–15.
73. Assmann and Sung, *Deus em Nós*, 25–26.
74. Ibid., 59.
75. Ibid., 77–89.
76. Ibid., 93.

through subject-to-subject relationships, has the potential of rupture, as it helps to raise questions about structural justice.[77]

The political-economic approach of the new generation of liberationists has changed significantly since the days of the movement's conception. This is so not only as a result of the changing context of Latin America, but also due to developments in the social sciences—the primary dialogue partner of LALT. For the purposes of this work, it is important to notice the increased proximity between North Atlantic Evangelicalism and LALT made possible by this approach. If LALT and North Atlantic Evangelicalism were at odds regarding the need for a market system, that is no longer the case. Though LALT has clear socialist leanings, the democratic, non-totalitarian, non-communist characteristics of its socio-economical positions are now fully developed. General disagreements between capitalists and democratic socialists are still significant, but the strong antagonism between the once heavy neoliberal convictions of NAEvs in general and the liberationists call for rupture with the market system is no longer there.

## Violence, Revolution, and Just War

As mentioned above, another recurrent criticism against LALT is its endorsement of violence. The inconsistency of the general North Atlantic Evangelical stance in relation to violence is that it usually rejects LALT's endorsement of violence, while at the same time supporting the militaristic endeavors of the United States. It is not difficult to see this inconsistency in evangelicals who condemn any revolutionary discourse as heretical but celebrate vigorously the American Revolution—especially in the traditionally nationalistic worship service of the Fourth of July. It is possible to argue theologically, as Hundley appears to do, that one does not need to be a pacifist to condemn the generally revolutionary discourse of early LALT; for just war theory cannot legitimize a "just revolution." As we will see below though, Hundley's argument is contested; however, even if Hundley is right, he can only partially justify the militaristic leanings of American evangelicals—not the vigorous celebration of the American independence. For if, as Hundley argues, the "biblical position" does not warrant for armed revolt against the state,[78] then the American Revolution was an ungodly event and

77. Ibid., 96.
78. Hundley, *Radical Liberation*, 48.

should be condemned as such—something very few non-pacifist, American evangelicals are willing to do.

The argument for the impossibility of the legitimation of just revolution by just war theory has not gone uncontested. The questions that surround the issue of just revolution are, to a great extent, connected to what just war theorists call "legitimate authority." Though it is undeniable that such theorists agree that, in most cases, only the nation-state has the legitimate authority to wage war, some argue that a few exceptions apply. According to Oliver O'Donovan, armed revolution is

> . . . more difficult to justify than war against external power. Yet on the judicial model revolution should be justifiable on precisely the same terms as foreign war, namely that if a government's authority erodes, there is a judicial vacuum that may be filled informally by any party acting in defense of conspicuous right.[79]

For O'Donovan

> . . . an act of ordered rebellion is itself the first step out of the mentality of denial, positing a new political order which agents of rebellion accept the responsibility of bringing about. To say this much, of course, is not to issue a general license to rebellion; it is simply to establish the ground on which rebellion, but not terrorism, might possibly lay claim to authority.[80]

O'Donovan's arguments clearly open the possibility of just war theory supporting revolution, as long as a few prerequisites are met.

Daniel Bell also provides helpful insight on the issue of just revolution. Looking at the history of just war theory, Bell states that:

> . . . modernity ceded to nation-states a monopoly on violence and the right to declare war does not mean that either that monopoly or that right went entirely unchallenged. Even before the right to wage war was lodged solely in the hands of the nation-state, in the Middle Ages the question of revolution was raised. And the issue of a just or legitimate revolution continued to be pressed in the modern world. If anything, the question of the legitimacy of revolution has intensified in the modern world as anticolonial movements emerged and as peoples rose up against oppressive regimes and brutal tyrants.[81]

79. O'Donovan, *Just War*, 26–27.
80. Ibid., 31.
81. Bell, *Just War*, 103.

Evangelicals and Liberation Revisited

Bell also identifies in Aquinas's teaching on the sin of sedition an exception to the sole autonomy of the nation-state to instigate just armed conflict. In doing so, Bell reveals that there are openings to the possibility of a just revolution deep within the tradition of the Church. Following Aquinas's teaching, Bell thinks one can argue that whenever the governing authorities become tyrannical and cease to promote the common good, they are guilty of sedition. According to Bell,

> In such a situation there is no sedition in disturbing a government if it can be done without giving rise to even greater harm. In fact, Aquinas notes, it is the tyrant who is actually guilty of sedition, precisely for betraying his office and attacking the common good.[82]

O'Donovan's and Bell's arguments clearly show that just revolution is indeed an option. Contrary to Hundley's opinion, just war theory leaves the possibility of justifiable revolt open, and consequently makes the case that legitimate authority is not necessarily entrusted solely to nation-states.

In the context of early LALT, violent governments that had their legitimacy questioned for being dictatorial, tyrannical, oppressive, and unjust were the rule rather than the exception. Though most early liberationists assumed that the revolutionary movements they supported were just causes and consequently never explicitly used just war theory to justify their option, an argument that just war theory possibly warrants such commitment can nonetheless be made. Provided this is the case, non-pacifists NAEvs cannot criticize LALT's endorsement of violence on the basis of just war theory with any consistency.

## Conclusion

This chapter attempted to bring Evangelicalism and LALT closer together by arguing that the general perception of LALT by NAEvs, for the most part, needs to take into consideration the developments of LALT. These developments include but are not limited to a more nuanced use of Marxism, the recognition of the necessity of the market, and the significant abandonment of revolutionary language. Furthermore, I attempted to show that even in the early, more revolutionary works of LALT, a concept of "just revolution" could have been developed and, consequentially, that a contradiction between non-pacifists NAEvs and LALT regarding their

---

82. Ibid., 106.

position on violence was never necessary. In light of these developments in LALT, Evangelicalism and LALT have not only grown closer together in their socio-political commitments, but also that they no longer need be perceived as contradictory when it comes to these issues.

# 5

## Church, World, and Salvation: A Case Study on James McClendon Jr. and Gustavo Gutierrez

THE RELATIONSHIP BETWEEN CHURCH and world is an important aspect of any theology. Explicitly or not, a theologian's understanding of the relationship between these realms is closely connected to major components of his or her theology especially with respect to soteriology, hamartiology, eschatology, and Christology. Its importance, therefore, goes beyond ecclesiology as one's articulation of church-world interaction affects and is affected by several aspects of any consistent theological construction. Avery Dulles, in his work on comparative ecclesiology, *Models of the Church*, highlights the centrality of this concept as he argues that the relationship between different faith groups is in large part determined by one's ecclesiological presuppositions.[1] Though it is beyond the scope of this chapter to analyze the extent to which a particular understanding of church-world relationship conditions or is conditioned by other particular doctrines, it is important to acknowledge the centrality and breadth of the topic so as to forestall any impression that the following observations are intended to exhaust the implications of a such complex subject.

This chapter will begin by presenting the concept of church-world relationship in the theologies of James McClendon Jr. and Gustavo Gutierrez. These two very distinct theologians, the first a North American Baptist evangelical and the latter a Latin American Catholic liberationist, developed approaches to the issue at hand that are widely dissimilar. I will focus on one of McClendon's major work—namely, the first volume of his

---

1. Dulles, *Models of the Church*, 3.

Systematic Theology and on Gutierrez's first and most important book *A Theology of Liberation*. It is important to point out that while Gutierrez's view is to a significant extent paradigmatic for LALT, McClendon's position is not necessarily so for evangelicals. When it comes to their understanding of the church, Latin American liberationists are considerably more homogeneous than evangelicals. However, McClendon was chosen to represent an evangelical view mainly because of his reputation as a systematic theologian—a reputation that reaches beyond evangelical circles.

After presenting the issue of church-world relationship according to these thinkers, I will deal with the subject of salvation, which I take to be closely connected to the relationship between church and world according to these two approaches. Finally, I will conclude by treating the question of the compatibility between the evangelical and the liberationist approach, which is the main concern of this work.

## Church and World According to James McClendon Jr.: An Evangelical Approach

In the first of his three-volume systematic theology James McClendon, Jr. presents his understanding of "how the church must live to be truly the church."[2] The unusual move of placing ethics at the forefront of his theology comes both from the conviction that the three parts of Christian systematic theology (apologetics, doctrine, and ethics) are ultimately interdependent and from pedagogical concerns, namely, that beginning students of theology may find ethics to be a more suiting starting point than "philosophical prolegomena."[3] McClendon's most significant theological influences were Karl Barth, John Howard Yoder, and Stanley Hauerwas;[4] thus, it is no surprise that he develops an approach to ethics that is particularistic,[5] Anabaptist,[6] and narratival.[7]

The post-foundationalist tendencies of McClendon's work are responsible for many of its peculiarities; for instance, his ethics does not attempt to

---

2. McClendon Jr., *Ethics*, 43.
3. Ibid., 40.
4. See Preface.
5. Ibid., 38–39.
6. Ibid., 33.
7. Ibid., 36–37.

provide values or principles that carry universal weight.[8] Rather, it focuses on the "discovery, understanding, and creative transformation of a shared and lived story, one whose focus is Jesus of Nazareth and the kingdom he claims."[9] McClendon's approach, therefore, claims to be true only in relationship to the particular story of the Christian narrative. The particular nature and narrative style of McClendon's Baptist approach to ethics considers the relationship between church and world to be fundamental[10] Out of the many significant features of McClendon's ethics, it is this relationship that will be analyzed in this section.

There are many facets of the issue of church/world relationship in McClendon's theology. Though his understanding of "church" finds a fairly coherent definition in his work, "world" is more ambiguous both in its meaning and in its relationship to the church. Nevertheless, the tension between church and world is clear in McClendon's theological approach. This brief assessment will focus on two connected but distinct features of McClendon's presentation of church/world interaction:

1. The oppositional reality of the two realms.
2. The view of the church as "redeemed culture," a term that McClendon uses to name the mediating structure that stands between our impulses and the actions they produce.

## Church and World as Opposed Realities

At the outset of his systematic theology, McClendon states that the relationship between church and world is central to theological reflection. After saying that theology is a struggle because "hard truth is not available without hard struggles,"[11] he goes on to say that

> The struggle begins with the humble fact that the church is not the world. This means that Christians face an interior struggle, inasmuch as the line between church and world passes right through each Christian heart. It nevertheless means that the standpoint, the basic point of view, the theology of the church is not the standpoint, basic point of view, theology of the world. The church's story

---

8. Ibid., 332–47.
9. Ibid., 330.
10. Ibid., 17.
11. Ibid.

> will not interpret the world to the world's satisfaction. Hence there is a temptation for the church to deny her "counter, original, spare, strange" starting point in Abraham and Jesus and to give instead a self-account or theology that will seem true to the world on the world's own terms. [. . .] conspiring to conceal the difference between church and world, we may in short run entice the world, but we will do so only by betraying the church.[12]

Thus, McClendon begins his work by presenting a view that focuses on the difference between church and world, a difference that is constitutive of the identities of both. McClendon argues that the world enters Christians as temptation for their true sociality is the church.[13] In this approach, the allegiance of the Christian should be solely with the church and in opposition to the world for these two structures oppose each other.

The confrontational relationship between church and world is clear in McClendon's approach. When talking about the need for an organic link between individual and social ethics, McClendon states that

> . . . for Christians the connecting link between the embodied ethics of each disciple and the communal ethics of the church confronting society, between the moral self and the morals of society, is to be found in the body of Christ that is the gathering church. [. . .] It is in such radical gatherings that directives for the pilgrimage of each end a shared witness to the outside world appear.[14]

For McClendon, the church confronts the world as part of its mission as a witness. In other words, part of what the church must do in order to be the church is dependent on the difference between church and world. To close the gap between these two realities is to threaten the church's very mission, the mission that gives the church part of its meaning. This confrontation seems to be supported by Scripture as it "confronts its readers with another world and asks if it is not in truth their world; it confronts them with another hope than their own hopes, and thus teaches them to ask, 'What wait I for? My hope is in thee.'"[15] McClendon's approach has redemptive purposes, namely, the regeneration of the world; nevertheless, it also and most importantly serves the purpose of supporting the church's own identity as non-world. For McClendon, the church is

12. Ibid., 17–18.
13. Ibid., 163–64.
14. Ibid., 214.
15. Ibid., 37.

> Exactly the realm in which responsibility to Jesus Christ is the hallmark of discipleship, so in it the call to be "responsible" can only be defined in terms of Christ's Lordship over all, not by any worldly measurement that for the time being sets him aside. The great temptation for today's disciples may be to feel "responsible" to the world as worldlings perceive it, even while withdrawing from the absolute claim of Jesus Christ's lordship.[16]

Therefore, the world does not set the agenda for the church's strategy but it is the church's sense of faithfulness to Christ that drives both the motivation and the method of witness it must adopt. The fact that McClendon is convinced that theology "properly culminates" in the question about faithfulness to Christ[17] supports the idea that in his theology, witness (which for him seems to be the most clear expression of Christian concern for the world) is a practice that must be done not with the world, but with faithfulness to Christ as its primary concern.

In *Doctrine*, McClendon makes this clear as he argues that it is the proclamation of the gospel that makes condemnation possible. McClendon thinks that, "The gospel puts recipients of our witness for Christ at great risk even as it offers them great gain"[18] but the fact that it is the church's witness that can bring damnation to non-Christians should not hinder the church's missionary impulse for Christians "are at equal risk if (they) fail faithfully to render the witness."[19] Statements such as these seem to indicate that McClendon's concern for the state of non-Christians is seen in light of his understanding of discipleship. In this understanding, the primary motivation for evangelism seems to be obedience to and right relationship with Christ. In this approach, concern for non-Christians is apparently secondary.

## The Church as Redeemed Culture

In McClendon's theology the world of the Christian community, a world that is identified by Scripture, is a strange world.[20] By participating in this different world in which obedience to the lordship of Christ is normative Christians enter into a new sociality, in other words, a new culture. Sin,

16. Ibid., 233.
17. Ibid., 34.
18. McClendon Jr., *Doctrine*, 131.
19. Ibid., 131.
20. Ibid., 337.

## Church, World, and Salvation

for McClendon, is not a bodily necessity, but it is a result of the culture that gives shape and guidance to one's drives, needs, and instincts. When presenting his ideas concerning the morality of the body, McClendon states the following:

> Consider the hypothesis that (1) our embodied selves are equipped by their Creator with certain characteristics drives, or impulses, or instincts, such as the drives to sex and aggression; (2) that we are furnished as well with certain related, determinate needs for companionship and prayer; and (3) that in the adventure in which we seek to meet these needs and cope with these drives, our selves acquire a range of feelings and may develop relevant powers of judgment—moral feelings and moral judgment, constituting the moral equipment or capacities of the body. Certainly it is not Christians alone who possess such drives, needs and capacities; evidently others do also. Nor is any Christian devoid or exempt, by virtue of Christ's grace, from such embodied drives, needs, or capacities. Yet, [. . .] the manner in which we participate in the common lot displays the Christian way; our share in the created order is shaped by our share in Jesus Christ—who also possessed these native drives, natural needs, and nascent resources of the body.[21]

For him, the fundamental problem is not the body itself, but what mediates the body's drives, what stands between instincts and action, namely, culture. This is the reason why McClendon can say that

> . . . there can be no surrender of Christian ethics to those who in Manichaean fashion regard the body's drives or instincts as the enemy of morality—or even as its mere material base, neither good nor evil. "God saw all that he had made, and it was very good," not least "human beings in our image, after our likeness" (Gen 1:31, 26). Granted, human nature is fallen and sinful; we here take up the standpoint of that same nature redeemed into Christian discipleship, reconciled to its created environment.[22]

By arguing that our instincts are identical to those of Christ and that redemption does away with the necessity of sin and consequently opens the possibility of sinlessness, he transfers to the culture that mediates one's actions the responsibility of guiding one's actions properly. Therefore, sinless life is possible insofar as the culture that guides one's instincts does it appropriately, for, as McClendon states, "the phenomenon of 'original' or basic sin

21. McClendon Jr., *Ethics*, 97.
22. Ibid., 98.

in human nature is connected not simply to bestial or animal drives of sex or aggression, but to the historic and variable forms of human culture."[23]

The images of the Christian community as "redeemed culture" and of the world as "fallen culture" are central to McClendon's ethics. It is important to notice that for him authentic Christianity is communal as "the content of Christian faith, or for that matter any faith that must be lived out, not just thought out, is best expressed in the shared lives of its believers; without such lives, that faith is dead."[24] The importance of this redeemed culture lies in the fact that it is in it that Christians must live and through it that they must interpret reality. In yet another expression of the oppositional relationship between church and world McClendon says that

> . . . the world is not Christian; there is fallenness and rebellion and ruin enough here. But the eyes through which we Christians see the world are redeemed eyes; it is through these eyes that we must be trained to look if we would see without double or narrow vision. To say that the way Jesus sees the organic world is normative for our seeing may be too cryptic for clarity, but if it reminds us that Christians have no moral Lord save Christ, it is beyond question a good motto."[25]

Here, as in other above cited quotes, one can detect that the extent to which redemption is accomplished in history is central. McClendon claims to take fallenness seriously, but redemption even more seriously.[26] It is exactly this issue that puts McClendon in opposition to other Christian ethicists. For him, while neo-orthodox ethics is pessimistic in its view of the human condition,[27] the Niebuhrian approach "is too grimly realistic in (its) assessment of the revolutionary possibilities of Christian community; (its) 'realism' overlooks the new life in Christ."[28]

What is already implicit in *Ethics* becomes explicit in the second volume of McClendon's systematic theology. In *Doctrine*, after developing his argument for the inappropriateness of the doctrine of original sin as understood by Augustine and by the Reformers, McClendon argues for

23. Ibid., 101.
24. Ibid., 119.
25. Ibid., 96.
26. Ibid., 95.
27. Ibid., 92–93.
28. Ibid., 168.

his understanding that sin is socially transmitted.[29] He says that his understanding of sin "denies that we can be guilty of others' sins; nevertheless we can suffer their consequences."[30] Here it becomes evident where McClendon thinks sin resides: in culture. In his understanding, to say different is to ascribe to Jesus Christ a nature that is not authentically human. He says that

> The biblical testimony contradicts those modern theologians who treat sin as creaturely limitation, a necessary feature of our created sensuous nature or will, or as a corollary of finite being, or as a paradoxically inevitable but not necessary circumstance growing form "man's involvement in nature and his transcendence over it." These readings of the human condition have the unhappy consequence of diminishing the possibilities of the new that comes in Christ. In the name of a doctrine of creation some have thus drained the good news of actual goodness. Consequently, they also make it more difficult to interpret the true humanity of Jesus Christ. If sin is simply human nature, what sort of nature is his?[31]

Thus, in McClendon's theology, in order for Christians to be able to affirm Jesus's authentic humanity, they must also affirm that sinful habits are not necessary for those who are followers of Christ and consequently are a part of a redeemed culture.

In summary, McClendon's narrative ethics has a central concern with culture, a word that he uses to name the structure that mediates human impulses in either negative/worldly ways or in positive/redeemed ways. As seen above, it is not without importance that McClendon states at the very beginning of his theology that church and world are opposing realities. His understanding of embodiment lays the groundwork for the definitive role that culture plays in channeling human drives toward righteous/Christian or sinful/worldly actions. For him, the church expresses the lifestyle of a redeemed culture, a lifestyle that is manifested in communities that participate in Christ's story. On the other hand, the "world" is a fallen culture, a culture that channels human impulses and drives toward sinful living.

---

29. McClendon Jr., *Doctrine*, 128–29.
30. Ibid., 129.
31. Ibid., 124.

## Church and World According to Gustavo Gutierrez: The Liberationist Approach

Responding to the turbulent context of mid twentieth-century Latin America, Peruvian priest Gustavo Gutierrez wrote, as mentioned above, the book that came to be known as one of the most important works on Latin American Liberation Theology. In *A Theology of Liberation*, Gutierrez sought to address the issue of oppression from the perspective of the only continent that is at the same time primarily Christian and poor. In the early seventies, when Gutierrez was writing the first edition of his *magnus opus*, his social location was turbulent and conflictive. The clergy of the Roman Catholic Church, with its history of siding with the ruling classes of Latin America, was divided among those who wished to keep their commitment to the status quo and those who wished for a radical change in its mission, identity, and structure. Gutierrez sided with the latter group and consequently with leftist political movements that saw in political action an avenue for changing the situation of misery that plagued the whole continent. His commitment to transform the oppressive situation of his context influenced him into developing a secularizing theology where the relationship of church and world is understood quite differently than in McClendon's theology.

At the very beginning of *A Theology of Liberation*, Gutierrez already indicates that his theology presupposes a close connection between church and world. He says that his book attempts to provide a reflection that is based on

> ... the gospel and the experiences of men and women committed to the process of liberation in the oppressed and exploited land of Latin America. It is a theological reflection born of the experience of shared efforts to abolish the current unjust situation and to build a different society, free and more human.[32]

By "shared efforts" Gutierrez means efforts that are common to both Christians and non-Christians. Though he aims to "elucidate" the meaning of the experience of the growing number of Christians that have embraced the commitment to the process of liberation, such commitment in not primarily ecclesiastical, but it is done in conjunction with the many Latin Americans who "have already started along the path of a commitment to liberation."[33] This understanding seems to imply a strong point of unification between those in the church and those outside of it in the common

---

32. Gutierrez, *A Theology of Liberation*, xiii.
33. Ibid.

commitment for building a better society. For Gutierrez, liberation theology must maintain a "twofold fidelity: to the God of our faith and to the peoples of Latin America. Therefore we cannot separate our discourse about God from the historical process of liberation."[34] This section will look at two elements of Gutierrez's theology that highlight his view of church-world relationship, namely:

1. The commitment to the poor.
2. Gutierrez's understanding of human activity, salvation, and historical unity.

## Commitment to the Poor

Gutierrez's theology is admittedly "closely bound up" with historical situations that arose out of the context of his continent and that came to the attention of liberation theologians through their experiences with the poor.[35] Because, in Gutierrez's opinion, poverty is a condition that can be better diagnosed and challenged by approaches that were developed outside ecclesiastical confines, he turns to such approaches, among which the social sciences are the most prominent, so that he can get the best description of reality possible.[36] When speaking of the need of using different tools in order to better analyze social reality Gutierrez says that: "The tools used in this analysis vary with time and according to their proven effectiveness for gaining knowledge of social reality and finding solutions to social problems."[37] Though Gutierrez is aware of the need of having discernment when using such tools, they play a major role in his theology as they provide, to a large extent, the interpretation of reality that ultimately will guide the specific efforts of those who embrace the commitment to liberation. For him, the social sciences can serve as mediators that "help us to understand better where and how the Lord is challenging us as we face the life (and death) of our brothers and sisters."[38]

The role played by the experience of the poor in Gutierrez's theology cannot be understated. For him, authentic commitment to liberation can

---

34. Ibid., xviii.
35. Ibid., xxi.
36. Ibid., xxiii–xxv.
37. Ibid., xxiv.
38. Ibid., xxv.

only exist from within the "world of the poor"[39]; it is the life of the poor in general and of the Christian communities in particular that provide "the historical womb from which liberation theology has emerged."[40] This interaction with the world of the poor is what gives Gutierrez's theology its distinctiveness. His conviction of the necessary contextual nature of theology allows him to admit that his own theology "takes its coloring from (his) peoples, cultures, racial groups, and yet (he) use(s) it in an attempt to proclaim the universality of God's love."[41]

The experiences that gave rise to liberation theology are not "Christian experiences" but "human experiences." According to Gutierrez, the longing for liberation in the heart of the poor of Latin America is a sign of the acting presence of the Spirit in history; a fact that challenges the church to respond accordingly.[42] This commitment to the poor, which Gutierrez sometimes articulates in terms of solidarity, challenges the church to re-think its own concept of identity in relation to it; in other words, the experience of poverty relativizes and strengthens the church's self understanding.[43] Gutierrez argues that

> Today, perhaps more than at other periods, certain tendencies within the church make it necessary to strengthen our ecclesiastical identity in fidelity to the Lord and in the determination to serve those to whom we preach the word. But a proper involvement in the world of the poor by no means detracts from the church's mission; rather in such involvement the church finds its true identity as a sign of the reign of God to which all humans beings are called but to which the lowly and the "unimportant" have privileged spaces. Solidarity with the poor does not weaken the church's identity but strengthens it.[44]

In this approach one's solidarity with the poor, and consequently with the world which the poor are a part of, is an indispensable element of the church as it presents the church's "true identity" and helps guide its missionary impulse.

---

39. Ibid., xxx.
40. Ibid., xxxiii.
41. Ibid., xxxv.
42. Ibid., xxxviii.
43. Ibid., xlii–xliii.
44. Ibid.

## Human Activity, Salvation, and Historical Unity

Gutierrez's understanding of theology as "reflection on humankind, on basic human principles"[45] highlights the fact that, for him, the data which theology reflects on is not primarily "religious data" but "human, historical data."[46] Developing on Congar's works, Gutierrez states that

> "Instead of using only revelation and tradition as starting points, as classical theology has generally done, it must start with facts and questions derived from the world and from history." It is precisely this opening to the totality of human history that allows theology to fulfill its critical function vis-à-vis ecclesial praxis without narrowness.[47]

This critical function of theology, which can only be accomplished by the church's opening to the world, is what safeguards both the church and society from justifying a "given social or ecclesial order"[48] in an absolute manner. This opening to the world keeps the church focused on the always changing historical realities and thus able to re-think its commitments in light of new historical situations. As mentioned above, for Gutierrez, the theology of liberation is more a way of doing theology than a new theological theme. The peculiarity of this new way of theologizing is in its solidarity with the oppressed and in its openness to the world; Gutierrez states that "this is a theology which does not stop reflecting on the world, but rather tries to be part of the process through which the world is transformed."[49]

Gutierrez's focus on the participation of the church in world transformation highlights his approval of the participation of the church in socio-political action. According to him, in the Latin American context, it is inevitable for the church to have impact on the political realm; he asks, "Is the church fulfilling a purely religious role when by its silence or friendly relationships it lends legitimacy to a dictatorial and oppressive government?"[50] He then goes on to argue that the church must choose to use its influence to liberate the oppressed, not to perpetuate the status

---

45. Ibid., 9.
46. Ibid.
47. Ibid., 9–10.
48. Ibid., 10.
49. Ibid., 12.
50. Ibid., 40.

quo.⁵¹ This transformative impulse in Gutierrez's theology shows that his concern for the world is seen as a responsibility in ameliorating it.

The newfound self-understanding in which humanity sees itself as creative subjects is, according to Gutierrez, a positive development that drives us to redefine the relationship of humanity to God. He argues that theology evolved beyond the profane-sacred/temporal-spiritual axis and that consequently God's call to salvation is heard universally in history; according to him:

> This affirmation of the single vocation to salvation, beyond all distinctions, gives religious value in a completely new way to human action in history, Christian and non-Christian alike. The building of a just society has worth in terms of the Kingdom, or in more current phraseology, to participate in the process of liberation is already, in a sense, a salvific work.⁵²

Again, it is the participation in the process of liberation, a process that is, to a great extent, defined in worldly terms through the social sciences, that names fidelity to God's call. In this approach, effectiveness and faithfulness are closely linked. It is the Lord who calls the church to be in solidarity with the world but, on the other hand, worldliness is a necessary condition for and authentic relationship "between humanity and God."⁵³ Such view has significant ramifications for the church. Gutierrez says that:

> In the first place, rather than define the world in relation to the religious phenomenon, it would seem that religion should be redefined in relation to the profane. The worldly sphere appears in fact ever more consistent in itself. [. . .] On the other hand—on a very concrete level in which we are particularly interested—if formerly the tendency was to see the world in terms of the Church, today almost the reverse is true: the Church is seen in terms of the world. In the past, the Church used the world for its own ends; today many Christians—and non-Christians—ask themselves if they should, for example, use the influence of the Church to accelerate the process of transformation of social structures.⁵⁴

Here it is clear that for Gutierrez the relationship between church and world is dynamic and interrelated; by arguing that the church should

51. Ibid.
52. Ibid., 46
53. Ibid., 42.
54. Ibid.

be redefined in relation to the profane, Gutierrez delegates to the world the responsibility of shaping the church's mission and consequently part of its identity.

The mission of the church that is in solidarity with the poor is accomplished through the implementation of several practices. First, the church must exercise what Gutierrez calls "prophetic denunciation,"[55] which is the denunciation by the church of oppressive social structures. Secondly, the church must engage in "conscienticizing evangelization," a form of evangelization that makes the evangelized aware of his or her condition as oppressed. Furthermore, the church must assume poverty and stop benefiting from the support of the ruling classes. Finally, the church and the clergy must make profound changes in its structures so that they can better reflect the Latin American situation.[56]

Gutierrez is convinced that authentic Christianity calls for a response to the Latin American situation, a response that requires commitment to the process of liberation. On a fundamental level, however, the goal of the liberationist movement goes beyond the establishment of a particular form of religious expression or government as it focuses on the creation of a new humanity.[57] In this process the focus is not a preoccupation with "quantitative salvation," that is, a spiritualized form of salvation that sees this life as a test for the life to come, but "qualitative salvation," which is "the communion of human beings with God and among themselves."[58] It is this communion that gives force to the human self-generation that initiated in the work of creation and now continues to take place in history. According to Gutierrez

> . . . when we assert that humanity fulfills itself by continuing the work of creation by means of its labor, we are saying that it places itself, by this very fact, within an all-embracing salvific process. To work, to transform this world, is to become a man and to build the human community; it is also to save. Likewise, to struggle against misery and exploitation and to build a just society is already to be a part of the salving action, which is moving towards its complete fulfillment. All this means that building the temporal city is not simply a stage of "humanization" or "pre-evangelization" as was held in theology until a few years ago. Rather it is to become part of a saving process which embraces the whole of humanity and

55. Ibid., 68.
56. Ibid., 68–72.
57. Ibid., 81.
58. Ibid., 86.

all human history. Any theological reflection on human work and social praxis ought to be rooted in this fundamental affirmation.[59]

Salvation, in this perspective, is attained in engaging in activities that are not exclusively Christian but fundamentally "secular." It is in working for a new society that God's call is heard; a call that is, as mentioned above, universal and that does not need the mediation of the church.

The fact that Gutierrez sees salvation as being present in liberative praxis allows him to draw close lines between temporal progress and growth of God's kingdom. For him

> Temporal progress—or, to avoid this aseptic term, human liberation—and the growth of the Kingdom both are directed toward complete communion of human beings with God and among themselves. They have the same goal, but they do not follow parallel roads, not even convergent ones. The growth of the Kingdom is a process which occurs historically in liberation, insofar as liberation means a greater human fulfillment. [. . .] Without liberating historical events, there would be no growth of the Kingdom.[60]

This close connection between liberation and salvation, between temporal progress and growth of the Kingdom, when paired with Gutierrez's affirmation that "When justice does not exist, God is not known; God is absent;"[61] and with his identification of conversion to the Lord with a form of conversion to the neighbor that includes socio-economic, cultural, and political aspects makes clear that for him the church shares strong commonalities with the "world." For Gutierrez, God's ultimate plan for humanity—integral liberation—takes place in history without the necessary mediation of the church; it is the church that must discern "the signs of times" and join the process of liberation in history if it is to be faithful to God's call.

According to Gutierrez, the church must take into consideration the "mediation of the consciousness of the 'other'—of the world in which (its) presence occurs" so that its own consciousness is appropriate and it does not develop into a rigid, ecclesiocentric consciousness. Though Christians can reveal things to the world once they have God's special revelation, the church must also "allow itself to be inhabited and evangelized by the world." It is Gutierrez's conviction that "the Church is not non-world; it is humanity

---

59. Ibid., 91.
60. Ibid., 104.
61. Ibid., 111.

itself attentive to the Word." The church is not the exclusive administrator of God's blessings, of God's salvific acts; for Gutierrez, the main focus of the Church should be on social transformation, a transformation of humanity into a new humanity, a transformation of the world into a just society. His understanding implies a relationship between church and world where there is a great deal of collaboration. The world helps define the church's identity and the church uses its influence to assist in the process of accomplishing God's goal for humanity.

## A Brief Comparison of Two Somewhat Opposing Views

The differences between McClendon's and Gutierrez's understandings of the relationship between church and world are considerable. As shown above, while McClendon focuses on the difference between church and world, Gutierrez focuses on their similarities. For McClendon, the difference between these two realms is so striking that theological reflection itself must start with the acknowledgement of the conflictive relationship between them. Gutierrez, on the other hand, starts by stating his dual commitment: to the Lord and to the people of Latin America. While the North American Baptist seems to understand the relationship between the two realms as conflictive, the Latin American Catholic sees the same relationship as cooperative.

When it comes to defining the church's identity, McClendon says bluntly that the church must not attempt to define itself in the world's terms; rather, the church must emphasize its otherness, its strange nature. The church as the community of God's people is a strange world to which the believer is invited to enter by way of Scripture. In this understanding, the authenticity of one's fidelity to Christ is not evaluated by any worldly standard. For McClendon, the world enters the Christian as temptation; therefore, the term "world" carries a necessarily negative connotation. It is the world that mediates human impulses negatively, making sin possible; on the other hand, the church as redeemed community mediates the same impulses positively, making sinlessness possible.

By contrast, Gutierrez ascribes to the world the responsibility of guiding the church's mission and strategy. In being open to the world and therefore defining its identity in relation to specific historical situations, the church is always in a process of self-definition. Though the church can rely on its function as signifier of God's love for humanity for a more stable concept of identity, the specific form in which this love is signified is open, contingent upon the world's demands as interpreted by the social sciences in vogue. This openness to the world, however, is understood by Gutierrez in terms of fidelity to God. Because God acts in history, calling all to a salvation that is more clearly manifested in the doing of justice, God's will can be identified in history. This is why Gutierrez sometimes refers to his theology as a theology of the "signs of time." As God acts in history, faithfulness to God requires that a reliable interpretation of reality is appropriated so that the church can discover what it must do in response to God's call.

Out of the many differences between McClendon's and Gutierrez's understanding of the relationship between church and world, two interconnected issues stand out, namely, the issue of identity and the issue of fidelity to the Lord. At the center of their views, questions about what the church is and about what the church must do in order to be faithful to Christ are asked. Their approaches should not be differentiated by using the often mentioned dichotomy between faithfulness and effectiveness for both of these theologians see these two characteristics as interrelated. While for McClendon effectiveness must be measured in terms of faithful discipleship, for Gutierrez faithful discipleship is manifested in the struggle for effective social change.

When it comes to the issue of identity, the most significant positive feature of McClendon's counter-cultural approach is that it gives the church a stable way for self-identification. McClendon's narrative and particularistic, baptist approach is confident that the gospels identify believers as disciples in the story of God's people. Defining the church's identity and mission is a process of discovering and understanding in which Christians find in Scripture what the church is. The identity of the church is, therefore, not perceived as being dictated from the outside but as coming out of the narrative of the followers of Christ. Though critics may point out that such immediate approach neglects the distance between the Bible and contemporary interpreters, McClendon's embrace of a strong sense of identification with the biblical narratives reinforces the self-understanding of the Christian community.

Negatively, McClendon runs the risk of defining the church's identity antithetically and consequently focusing primarily in negating the world rather than on affirming the church and its responsibility to the world. In other words, McClendon's approach can fall on the trap of focusing on what the church is against rather than what the church is for by emphasizing the negation of culture to the detriment of the affirmation of the church. This risk is evident in the very beginning of McClendon's work where he, before defining either church or world, declares the opposing relationship between them.

For Gutierrez the risk is that by affirming openness to the world too strongly, he leaves no stable identifier for the church to use for its self-definition. The identity of the church is, for him, better defined in functional terms. The authentic church is the church of the oppressed; it is comprised of those who are in solidarity with the poor and against the evil structures that oppress them. Though this approach shows a strong concern for the world, it does so at the expense of a strong sense of identity, a sense of identity that is not so dependent on historically conditioned perceptions of reality.

The main points of tension between these two theologies, the issues of identity and fidelity, present peculiar challenges to each approach. For McClendon, the main issue is the perceived lack of sincere, incarnational concern for the world. Though McClendon articulates his concern for the world in terms of witness, it is this witness that makes possible for non-Christians to be condemned. On the other hand, the Christian's ability of being in good standing with Christ is contingent upon the Christian's witness; in this perspective, as mentioned above, one's discipleship takes precedence over one's concern for the "Other."

Gutierrez's approach does not necessarily solve the issue presented by McClendon as it also identifies authentic Christianity with a specific attitude, namely, commitment to the process of liberation. In his theology, concern for the Other is not only the highest form of discipleship but it is what enables one to be a participator in God's historical activity. Therefore, Gutierrez's emphasis is on transformative action, action for the world from within the world, shows a greater concern for humanity as whole. Furthermore, his articulation of God's universal call de-emphasizes the ecclesiastical administration of salvation, showing that his main focus is not as much on other-worldly salvation as it is in social transformation.

## Salvation Proper

McClendon's and Gutierrez's understanding of church-world relationship already point to some key aspects of their soteriology. Though McClendon is not among conservative evangelicals, his concept of salvation resembles conservatives in its exclusivist-eschatological focus. Unlike many of his evangelical peers, McClendon is an inclusivist up to a certain point, namely, the proclamation of the gospel; because for him the possibility of damnation comes with the hearing of the gospel message, wherever the gospel is preached, the hearer's acceptance or rejection to that message will determine his or her fate. It is difficult, however, to determine how McClendon understands salvation happens before gospel proclamation; how people are in "good standing" with God before an "evangelical conversion" experience.

For Gutierrez and the great majority of Latin American liberationists, salvation is understood in inclusivist-historical terms. God's call to humanity is heard by all in history and those who respond positively by entering God's plan of implementing a more just society are accepted in good standing. Though the ideal is for one to be a full-fledge, confessional Christian, acceptance or rejection of the gospel does not necessarily determine one's fate partially because the integrity of the proclaimer is taken into consideration when assessing the authenticity of the proclamation.

Vatican II, whose teachings are seen by Gutierrez as needing mediation for their implementation in the Latin American context but are never contradicted by him, is inclusivist in nature. Gutierrez assumes this inclusivity in his theology. The Council, however, qualifies its inclusivity and limits it to cases of "inculpable ignorance."[62] What counts as inculpable ignorance can be broadly understood. British scholar Stephen Bullivant, a specialist in the theology of unbelief, recently pointed out what the council meant by inculpable ignorance. According to Bullivant

> What Vatican II seems to have intended by inculpable ignorance is, therefore, in substantial agreement with what, in the 16th century, Las Casas and Vitoria meant by invincible ignorance. That is not, of course, to ignore the major disparities between their respective *Sitz im Leben:* many of Vatican II's *ignorantes* would, presumably, have been brought up either within at least nominally Christian societies, or would have had at least some acquaintance, however superficial, with Christianity. Differences aside, however, both Vatican II and the great Dominicans accept that (1) inculpable/invincible ignorance prevents unbelief from being sinful; and (2) this kind of ignorance may be prolonged, even after acquaintance with Christianity and the Church's proclamation, if the latter is either intrinsically insufficient or if Christians themselves fail *scandalously* (in the full, scriptural sense of the term) to live up to the name.[63]

To my knowledge, Gutierrez never addresses the issue of inculpable ignorance explicitly. However, the fact that he eventually became a Dominican, his appreciation for Bartolome de las Casas, and his characterization

---

62. Bullivant, "Sine Culpa?," 72.
63. Ibid., 81–82.

of the RCC in Latin America as an institution that historically supported the oppressive status quo make it reasonable to infer that he assumes that Latin Americans who resist Christianity can be characterized as being in state of inculpable ignorance.

If the above inference holds water, the fundamental difference between McClendon's and Gutierrez's soteriology may be their understanding of what constitutes authentic gospel proclamation. While for McClendon, an American evangelical who lived in a place where Protestantism, the major expression of Christianity, is not generally perceived as a tool for political-economic oppression, Gutierrez's theology was developed in an environment where the RCC was seen as an ally of the conservative ruling class. Therefore, while McClendon's context may allow for the assumption that gospel proclamation in the sense of spoken evangelism automatically eliminates inculpable ignorance (a term which he may or may not be familiar with), Gutierrez's context calls for an opposite attitude, namely, the assumption that there is abundant reason for the resistance of gospel proclamation because of the proclaimer's failure to live up to the name of Christ. In other words, McClendon's context warrant an ecclesiology of trust , which may explain his optimistic view of the church and negative view of the world. Gutierrez's context, on the other hand, warrants suspicion of the RCC due to its history of supporting the elite, a fact that may explain his view of the world as an ally and of salvation as finding mediation in historical action, not in plain gospel proclamation. As evangelical theologian Ronald Sider noticed

> It is understandable that Black and Latin American theologians would be impressed by the fact that whereas most of the organized church regularly ignores the injustice that causes poverty and oppression, those who do care enough to risk their lives for improved conditions are often people who explicitly reject Christianity.[64]

Furthermore, some evangelical theologians developed their own version of inculpable ignorance.

Orlando Costas, for example, talks about authentic evangelization in ways that seem to allow for a defense of the teaching of inculpable ignorance. Costas says that

> To evangelize effectively in (the Latin American) situation it is necessary to overcome the historical contradictions that have characterized the proclamation of the gospel. The good news of

---

64. Sider, "An Evangelical," 314.

salvation cannot be announced with credibility without denouncing the surrounding sinful situation, nor can injustice, disobedience, and idolatry be denounced without announcing God's call to obedience, justification by faith, and reconciliation to God, neighbors, and nature. One cannot evangelize, either, if one is bound to sin in any of its dimensions or withdraws from the pain and suffering of those who are to be evangelized. Evangelization demands, above all things, authenticity. Therefore, in order to evangelize effectively, one must have experienced liberation from the power of sin and death, communion with God, neighbors, and the rest of creation, and be earnestly and passionately involved in the search for a just peace among the nations and their inhabitants.[65]

For Costas—as for those who along with Vatican II argue for the impossibility of evangelization without authentic, verifiable Christian living—either direct or indirect participation in oppression invalidates evangelization. Costas argues that his understanding of evangelization

... implies that it is impossible to bring good news of salvation in a poor and oppressed continent if one is allied to structures that disregard life and perpetuate injustice. To do so would be to perpetuate the contradiction between the sword and the cross. It would mean sharing the liberating message of the gospel with one hand and justifying domination and exploitation with the other.[66]

To Costas, evangelistic methods that are not consistent with the message of the Gospel and with "the God in whose name evangelization is done"[67] are, for the most part, inauthentic and, therefore, it is reasonable to infer that Costas, in order to be consistent, would agree with the affirmation that people who have heard and rejected the gospel message because it was preached by sources that have their authenticity explicitly questioned can be considered inculpably ignorant.

## Conclusion

This chapter examined an evangelical approach to the issues of church-world relationship and salvation and compared it to the general Latin American liberationist approach to the same issues with the goal of better understand the implications of both. However, the question of compatibility was only dealt

---

65. Costas, *Christ Outside the Gate*, 36–37.
66. Ibid., 37.
67. Ibid.

*Church, World, and Salvation*

with in passage. Above, it was suggested that part of the after-proclamation-exclusivism of McClendon's theology may partially be made possible by the general trust in Christianity that McClendon's context provides; a context in which the proclaimer usually does not incite automatic suspicion in his audience and therefore is able to perform authentic proclamation. In Gutierrez's context, however, the RCC is many times resisted among leftist, atheist Latin Americans for whom its testimony is made ineffective due to its history of allegiances that were detrimental to the continent's integral development. This means that rejection of gospel proclamation by Latin Americans may still be understood in terms of "inculpable ignorance;" a condition that is possibly equivalent to that of those who are positioned in McClendon's pre-proclamation-immunity. Therefore, it seems that context may explain a significant part of the apparent tension that exists between these two soteriologies.

When it comes to the issue of church-world relationship, McClendon's and Gutierrez's approaches seem harder to reconcile, but it must be noted that they are almost opposite in the spectrum of possible scenarios. To use H.R. Niebuhr's terms, while McClendon's position is "Christ-Against-Culture," Gutierrez's resembles the model that Niebuhr called "Christ the Transformer of Culture." As a testimony of the evangelical diversity on the topic one can mention, on one hand, Carl F. Henry's position that Christians should not force new structures upon society at large but need to be a new society, a position that seems to match McClendon's.[68] On the other hand, one can point to Ronald Sider, who not only fully accepts the doctrine of the preferential option for the poor, but who also agrees with the liberationists that knowing God necessarily involves being involved in the process of implementing justice in the world as an evangelical who seems to share greater common ground with Gutierrez's articulation of these issues.[69] Furthermore, Orlando Costas, a Latin American evangelical theologian, articulates the necessity of participation in the implementation of justice as a prerequisite for authentic evangelization and, therefore, seems to be in agreement with the argument that in Latin America, because of the historical oppressive position of the church, even those who have heard the gospel can be considered inculpably ignorant. Therefore, one can , in the Latin American context, include non-Christians who have heard the gospel among unreached groups, a move that would allow inclusivists to articulate their salvation in terms of response to the call of God in their consciences as liberationists often do.

68. Henry, "Liberation," 191.
69. Sider, "An Evangelical," 314–17.

# 6

# Christology

ACCORDING TO THE BRITISH evangelical Andrew Kirk, Christology is one of the major doctrinal gaps of LALT.[1] Though there could be some merit to this criticism, it may be more appropriate for evangelicals to see liberationist Christology as reductionistic or incomplete rather than heretical, as some evangelicals do. In order to argue for compatibility between evangelical Christology and the central teachings of liberationist Christology, I will present Leonardo Boff's Christology as a test case to show that the liberationist understanding of Christ can be generally affirmed by evangelicals—while still recognizing that Boff's christological ideas must be further developed.

## Leonardo Boff: A Liberationist Christology

Liberation theologian Jon Sobrino contends that Leonardo Boff was the first theologian who attempted to develop a Christology that reflected the Latin American context of the second half of the twentieth century.[2] Though some argue that Boff's Christology lacks originality because of its dependency on European theology,[3] a careful reading of Boff reveals that his engagement with European dialogue partners does not overshadow his own contributions to Christology. Despite that Boff's participation in the theological scene has diminished considerably, his Christology still

---

1. Kirk, *Liberation Theology*, 50.
2. Sobrino, *Christology*, 33.
3. Cook, "Jesus from the Other Side," 269.

## Christology

influences branches of Latin American Evangelicalism[4]—consequence of the fact that Latin American evangelicals realize the necessity of a Christology that reflects their context. Until Boff, it seems they were unable to develop a Latin American Christology from an evangelical perspective.[5]

This section analyzes Boff's Christology by looking at

1. Elements of Boff's deconstructionist approach to Scripture and traditional Christologies.

2. The meaning Boff ascribes to the person and work of Jesus Christ.

I will conclude by arguing that Boff's Christology is kenotic, Chalcedonian, and properly suited for the context in which it was developed.

## Scripture and Traditional Christologies

Boff's Christology prioritizes liberative praxis[6] over academic speculation.[7] His understanding of theology clearly shows his commitment to the cause of the poor.[8] For him, the role of theology is to give contextual shape to the experience of spiritual encounter with the Lord among the poor. Following the presupposition that theology arises out of a historical experience, Boff argues for the necessity of a contextual approach to Christology that seeks to:

1. Deconstruct traditional christological discourse in order to reveal its inadequacy for the Latin American context.

2. Present an image of Christ that reflects the Latin American condition.[9]

Boff's deconstruction of traditional Christologies is based upon the fact that, for him, every intellectual endeavor is "under the commanding influence of a 'horizon of interest'"[10] and that therefore, "there is no know-

4. Lopes, "A Hermenêutica," 1.

5. Heaney, *Contextual*, 170.

6. For a treatment of the use of the term "praxis" in Latin American Liberation Theology see Steven Mackey, "Praxis as the Context of Interpretation: A Study of Latin American Liberation Theology," in *Journal of Theology for Southern Africa* 24 (1978): 31–43 and John J. Markey, "Praxis in Liberation Theology: Some Clarifications," in *Missiology: An International Review* XXIII/2 (1995): 179–95.

7. Piar, *Jesus and Liberation*, 2.

8. Boff, "The Need for Political Saints," 370.

9. Piar, *Jesus and Liberation*, 2.

10. Boff, *Passion*, 1.

ing, no knowledge that is free from ideology."[11] This is not only true of post-apostolic theological construction but of Scripture itself, as, for Boff, "the Gospels are above all interpretation of the events rather than an objective and disinterested description of the historical Jesus of Nazareth."[12] Consequently, Boff's understanding of the nature of the Gospels and his view of traditional Christologies are of major importance for the deconstructive phase of his project.

### Boff's General Understanding of the Gospels

Boff approaches the Gospels with the presupposition that historical-criticism, though not objective, helps the interpreter better understand who Jesus was. Though Boff is aware that every "history" of Jesus will reflect the author's historical situation,[13] the Gospels—in spite of their confessional nature—can give a general idea of what Jesus was like for "it was the historical Jesus that motivated the christological process and the multiple interpretations"[14] given to the story of Jesus Christ. Building on Boff's presupposition, Sobrino clarifies that this historicist concern is based on the conviction that it is the historic life of Jesus that is the fullest revelation of the Christian God; furthermore, the historical Jesus approach seeks to balance two extremes:

1. The kerygmatic approach that devalues the Gospels' ability of proclaiming truth about Jesus.
2. The immediate approach that neglects the distance between text and interpreter.[15]

Despite Boff's interests in the historical Jesus, he does not militate against the "transcendent meaning of the passion and death of the Lord."[16] Instead he "seeks to supply the dimension constituted by the historical, political mediations—in fine, the underpinnings—of that religious,

---

11. Ibid.
12. Boff, *Jesus Christ*, 3.
13. Ibid.,5.
14. Ibid., 12.
15. Sobrino, *Christology*, 10–12.
16. Boff, *Passion*, 7.

transcendent meaning."[17] Because such an approach uses extra-biblical criteria in order to establish what is antecedent to the biblical text, it can be seen as subjective.[18] Boff is aware of the subjective character of his theology. He willingly admits that "whatever the theologian's image of Jesus, that will be the theologian's guide to exegetical discussions."[19] This view, however, is not a warrant for uncritical thinking. Boff believes that

> . . . a reading situated outside the New Testament will have to take on the task of an antecedent critique. It will have to maintain ongoing vigilance vis-a-vis the scope of the New Testament interpretation of the historical reality of the facts narrated. It will have to ask itself in all honesty: To what extent are the facts narrated the projection of an antecedent theological interpretation? And at the same time we shall have to ask ourselves at all times: To what extent does our own interest attempt to force the text to say more than it really says? To what extent are we projecting rather than assimilating?[20]

Therefore, Boff's approach is suspicious of theological constructions both inside and outside Scripture while also being self-critical. He accepts the historical-critical method, which was sanctioned by Vatican II,[21] but not without reservations. The Gospels can be trusted, but they are not devoid of contextual concerns; ultimately, what the Gospels announce is

> . . . the presence of a new reality: Jesus resurrected, victor over death, sin, and all that alienates the human person. Because of this they proclaim the presence of a new hope in the heart of history. It is not their primary intention to announce a new doctrine and a new interpretation of our relations to God.[22]

## Boff's Approach to Traditional Christologies

Suspicion of imported christological images is not unwarranted in Latin America. From Columbus's colonialist Christ to the more contemporary

17. Ibid.
18. Lopes, "A Hermenêutica," 5–6.
19. Boff, *Passion*, 25.
20. Ibid., 7–8.
21. Ibid., 25.
22. Boff, *Jesus Christ*, 18.

christological images of helpless infant and powerless, suffering victim, Latin Americans have been exposed to images that served detrimental social functions.²³ Boff reacts against images of Christ that may conflict with liberation from socio-political oppression. He says that

> The wealthy sectors of society in particular—the powers that be—have utilized the symbol of the cross and the fact of the redemptive death of Christ to demonstrate the need for suffering and death as part and parcel of human life. [. . .] This manner of discourse is extremely ambiguous and open to facile manipulation.²⁴

At the same time, Boff is not against such images *per se*, but only against their implementation in the Latin American context. According to him

> The rise of a Catholicism that is typical from LA should not provoke a schism. Pluralism is an expression of the richness of unity, it is not a threat. Today, Liberation Theology constitutes the most vigorous religious thinking of the Third World. The poor and those who are committed to them are thinking about their problems through the perspective of the poor not that of the rich.²⁵

It is clear that Boff criticizes other Christologies not as an attempt to develop a Christology that will replace them in every situation, but because of his conviction that any Christology must not confuse context with content. The three main arguments he presents against imported, unadapted Christologies are the following:

1. That they carry meanings that are irrelevant to the pressing situation in which the vast majority of Latin Americans live.
2. They do not serve to advance in the people the awareness that they are agents of their own liberation.
3. They serve as ideologies legitimizing the oppressive and exploitative situation in which the poor in Latin American have existed for centuries.²⁶

---

23. Heaney, *Contextual*, 158–59.
24. Boff, *Passion*, 2.
25. Boff, "La Iglesia," 98.
26. Piar, *Jesus and Liberation*, 49.

# Christology

## Jesus's Person and Work

Boff's Christology is not as much a presentation of new christological content as it is a peculiar way of accessing that content.[27] He states that there are five characteristics, five "primacies" that guide his work: namely,

1. The primacy of the anthropological element over the ecclesiastical, (which means that his focus is not the church but "the human person that it should help").[28]
2. The primacy of the utopian element over the factual (the former of which is more suited for motivating social transformation).
3. The primacy of the critical element over the dogmatic (a reaction against obsolete dogmas that are no longer appropriate).
4. The primacy of the social over the personal (which emphasizes structural evils over individual ones).
5. The primacy of orthopraxis over orthodoxy (placing ethical behavior above systematization).[29]

The specific content of Boff's Christology can be traced back to one or more of these "primacies," which are a statement of the commitments that give shape to Boff's understanding of Christ.

Boff's Christology attempts to show how liberative praxis is consistent with orthodoxy. His focus is on how to relate Christology to the lives of people living under oppression; therefore, since abstractions are not his main concern, there are speculative matters that are left unexplained.[30] Boff is aware of some of the criticisms that his theology will face, as he is also aware that no system is seamless; according to him, "every theology has its risks."[31]

As in other Liberation Christologies, Boff follows Vatican II in its affirmation that rational human beings can identify what is right and act accordingly, "which is why Christians can join with other rational human beings in the struggle against injustice and why theology must

---

27. Waltermire, *The Liberation*, 87.
28. Boff, *Jesus Christ*, 44.
29. Ibid., 44–48.
30. Piar, *Jesus and Liberation*, 17–18.
31. Boff, "O Interesse dos Pobres," 101.

necessarily be a second step."³² Jesus Christ does not "bring any cultural model in particular,"³³ but he realizes the messianic expectation of the human heart. Boff says that

> Jesus Christ is not an aberration within history. He represents the highest emergence of the dynamism that God himself placed in creation and especially in human beings. This dynamism is the basis of Christianity prior to Christ and independent of an explicit profession of faith in Jesus Christ. Christians are not simply ones who profess Christ with their lips but ones who, yesterday and today, live the structure and comportment that Christ lived: love, forgiveness, complete openness to God, etc . . . .³⁴

For him, God's proposal for a new life does not emerge specifically in Jesus, but within the human conscience; it is a universal proposal. This proposal happens "whenever conscience feels responsible and experiences a challenge to go out of itself, to accept the other, to assume the task."³⁵ This environment of constant divine proposal is what Boff calls "Christic Structure," a universal structure that precedes Jesus and was implemented by Christ in the act of creation. The importance of the incarnate Christ lies in the fact that in him

> . . . there is a qualitative jump within the history of salvation: For the first time, divine proposal and human response, word and reality, promises and realization, arrived at a perfect accommodation. In him, therefore, salvation was given in absolute and eschatological form. In him the dynamism and latent possibilities of all creation became concrete and achieved full clarification.³⁶

Therefore, Boff does not see the incarnate Christ only as an end, but as a starting point,³⁷ and as the event that motivates and warrants liberative praxis. It is with this praxis in mind that Boff interprets Jesus's person and work.

Boff is not interested in affirming Jesus's divinity *a priori*. Instead, he is more concerned with analyzing the process by which "Jesus became

---

32. Piar, *Jesus and Liberation*, 61.
33. Boff, *Jesus Christ*, 40.
34. Ibid., 247.
35. Ibid., 255.
36. Ibid., 43.
37. Ibid.

## Christology

recognized and proclaimed as divine."[38] Boff is convinced that focusing on the Christ of faith will produce views of the atonement that inevitably dehistoricize Jesus's work and strip his life of any soteriological significance.[39] Jesus's life, though important, does not prescribe the specifics of contemporary action. What is central in Jesus's life is "the validation of a nucleus of facts concerning the situation surrounding Jesus and his response to it."[40] Such responses, then, must be contextualized so that they are meaningful for the Latin American situation. Boff, however, does not accept charges of historical positivism or ethical relativism. Though Jesus's example does not lie in the particularity of his actions, there is an imperative in "the fundamental dispositions by which his actions are motivated, dispositions such as the preferential option for the poor, a critical and conflictive stance toward the ruling class, and a willingness to suffer for the cause of liberation."[41] Furthermore, in the incarnation, Jesus sets the example of the process by which men and women make such dispositions historically concrete.[42]

For Boff, though Jesus possessed a "messianic conscience," he never applied traditional eschatological titles to himself.[43] It was the primitive church that, guided by their own interests, added such titles after the resurrection.[44] This is not to say that the post-resurrection titles do not reflect who Jesus was;[45] nevertheless, Jesus was only considered God in the end of a long process of meditation by his followers.[46] Furthermore, Jesus acted spontaneously according to God's will; he did not know all the details of his life and death *a priori*.[47] He did regard himself as the eschatological prophet who "actualizes the new order that God shall momentarily introduce"[48]—namely, the kingdom of God—but at the same time, he was only progressively aware of his

---

38. Piar, *Jesus and Liberation*, 23.
39. Ibid., 27.
40. Ibid., 57.
41. Ibid., 62.
42. Ibid.
43. Boff, *Jesus Christ*, 13.
44. Ibid., 37.
45. Ibid., 52.
46. Ibid., 179.
47. Boff, *Passion*, 60–61.
48. Ibid., 45.

death, Boff contends:⁴⁹ "it was only on the cross that Jesus realized that his end was at hand—that he was really going to die."⁵⁰

Jesus's expectations were connected to the kingdom of God that he came to proclaim. He understood himself "not only as the herald of this exhilarating news, but as the agent of its actualization."⁵¹ Boff argues that Jesus's death is not more important than his life. According to Boff, the meaning that Jesus ascribed to his death is "the one ascribed to his life. Jesus understood life not as something to be lived and enjoyed for itself, but as something to be lived for the service to others."⁵² Consequently, redemption "does not depend on some mathematical point in Jesus' life, not even on the moment of his death. His death is redemptive only in its identity as part of his life."⁵³

In his earthly life, Jesus is depicted as an agent in the process of liberation from structural sin. First, he relativizes human self-sufficiency by de-absolutizing the cultic, legal, and religious forms that monopolize the route to salvation.⁵⁴ For Boff, "salvation comes by way of our neighbor. The purpose of religion is not to substitute for our neighbor, but to establish in us a permanent orientation to genuine love of the other."⁵⁵ Secondly, he creates a new solidarity by siding with the marginalized. Jesus also establishes the principle of respecting the freedom of others: As Boff argues, "[h]is assertions are not 'authoritative' but persuasive. He always leaves the other a space for freedom."⁵⁶ In fourth place, Jesus shows an inexhaustible capacity to bear up under conflict. This is an important characteristic for Boff, as he presupposes that conflict is inevitable in the struggle for the liberation from oppression. Finally, Jesus shows his acceptance of mortality—an acceptance of a death that was not sought after, but imposed. For Boff, the death of Christ was a crime—"not a requirement of the will of a God eager for the reparation of outraged honor, concerned for the aesthetics of the divine relationship with humanity."⁵⁷ His resurrection gives universality to

---

49. Ibid., 47.
50. Ibid., 52.
51. Ibid., 53.
52. Ibid., 63.
53. Ibid.
54. Ibid., 16–17.
55. Ibid.
56. Ibid., 18.
57. Ibid., 3.

# Christology

Jesus's liberationist project; it means "the victory of life, the victory of the rights of the oppressed, the victory of justice for the weak."[58]

## A Christology of Liberative Praxis

Despite the fact that Boff's Christology is "from below," he strongly affirms the Chalcedonian Creed. He says that his Christology does not "deny Jesus' divinity at any moment."[59] Instead, it affirms that "Jesus was God from the moment of his conception; but there was growth in self-consciousness and awareness of this reality."[60] In a clear endorsement of Chalcedon, Boff says that despite the fact that he follows the Franciscan, "from below" approach, the council "infallibly and irreformably, defined for Christian faith of all time to come the true humanity and the true divinity of Jesus Christ. In Jesus Christ, the oneness of the single divine person of the eternal Word, subsist two distinct natures, without division, without separation."[61] That in Boff's Christology Christ lacks attributes such as omnipresence, omnipotence, and omniscience only indicates that he has a kenotic understanding of Christ.

Arguing for the superiority of kenotic Christologies in explaining the hypostatic union is beyond the scope of this chapter; however, it is widely recognized that kenotic Christologies provide a valid interpretation of Chalcedon.[62] Kenotic Christology has to do with the idea that "in order to assume human nature without affecting an elevation of that nature above the limits proper to the human, it was necessary for the divine Logos to divest himself of certain divine attributes."[63] According to defenders of kenotic Christologies, however, a distinction must be made between essential and accidental attributes,[64] in which the attributes of omnipotence, omnipresence, and omniscience are understood as accidental.[65] Though Boff does not deal explicitly

---

58. Ibid., 68.
59. Boff, "La Iglesia," 98.
60. Ibid.
61. Boff, *Passion*, xi.
62. Davis, "Is Kenosis Orthodox?," 121.
63. McCormack, "Karl Barth's Christology," 246.
64 Some forms of kenotic Christologies, instead of holding that distinction, opt to defend the idea that Jesus Christ had all attributes but chose not to use them. For a defense of this position see Gregory A Boyd and Paul Eddy, *Across the Spectrum: Understanding Issues in Evangelical Theology* (Grand Rapids: Baker Academic, 2009).
65. Davis, "Is Kenosis Orthodox?," 116.

with these matters, he clearly presupposes them. Given both his affirmation of Chalcedon and his "from below" point of departure, it is reasonable to conclude that Boff's Christology is both kenotic and orthodox.

Considering the structurally oppressive condition of Latin America in the mid-to-late 1900s, Boff's attempt to construct a Christology that would foster liberative practices is commendable. In Latin America, it is widely agreed among Christian theologians in general that the traditional images of Christ have been detrimental to social action because of their tendency to sacramentalize suffering and powerlessness. Boff resists this tendency by ascribing a greater importance to Christ's liberating mission than to his death. For Boff, because Christ's death and resurrection serve the primary purpose of affirming Christ's redemptive life, oppressed people can look to Christ as one who warrants liberative action rather than as one who blesses unnecessary suffering.

## Liberation Christology and Evangelicals

Analyzing all the aspects in which Boff's account of liberationist Christology may be criticized by NAEvs is beyond the purpose of this book. It was already stated above that issues such as inclusivism, kenotic Christology, hermeneutics, theological construction, and theories of the atonement are widely discussed among evangelicals and are, therefore, contested subjects. The question with which this work is concerned is whether a liberationist Christology can be compatible with Evangelicalism. It is submitted here that a sympathetic reading of Boff allows one to answer this question affirmatively, but not without qualifications.

The above presentation of Boff's Christology attempted to show that, to a great extent, Boff understands his Christology as one that differs from other, more classical accounts mainly because of its emphasis. This is why Boff lays out his presuppositions in the form of five primacies. His Christology explicitly focuses on what Boff calls the anthropological, utopian, critical, social, and orthopraxis elements. That he goes out of his way to affirm the transcendent meaning of the passion and to celebrate the plurality of christological approaches confirms his eagerness to call attention to christological aspects that, in his view, have been neglected by traditional theology and must be brought back into the Christological mix—aspects such as the liberative element that is manifested in Jesus's life in general and in the political-liberative praxis that following Jesus in the Latin American

## Christology

context calls for in particular. Of course this is not exhaustive of all Christology; arguably Boff never intended it to be so. However, the central aspects that Boff emphasizes—namely, Jesus's active obedience, the moral influence of Jesus's death, Jesus's death as victory over evil, and the importance of following Jesus (though for Boff this following takes place in a contextualized form)—are indeed an integral part of evangelical christological accounts.

When it comes to the general evangelical christological stance, the centrality of substitutionary atonement cannot be understated—especially in conservative circles. However, if this theory of the atonement is assumed as the standard for orthodox, evangelical Christology, not only will many theologians who call themselves evangelicals be alienated from the movement, but alternative Christologies such as Boff's will very likely be dismissed without a fair hearing. Nevertheless, even conservative evangelicals recognize elements emphasized by Boff. In his *Systematic Theology,* Wayne Grudem affirms what he calls the "example theory" as true but incomplete.[66] James McClendon Jr., who does not embrace substitutionary atonement in the classical sense, incorporates elements of both the *Christus-victor* and the moral example theory into his own Christology.[67] Citing the Vatican II documents, Thomas Oden pictures Jesus's death as "an incomparable victory, not simply over suffering, but through suffering over evil."[68] Though Oden ascribes to substitutionary atonement, he also accepts the idea that Christ's death exercises a moral influence upon believing humanity.[69] British evangelical Andrew Kirk affirms that "[t]he formal statement of Christ's finality would not be disputed by any of the theologians of liberation."[70] Though Kirk is not persuaded by the articulations of liberation Christology with which he interacts, he realizes that Christ is not a marginal figure for liberation theologians. This is by no means an exhaustive list of evangelicals who, in one way or another, affirm elements emphasized by Boff. The problem, however, seems not to be what Boff affirms but what he denies.

Because Boff denies the necessity of Jesus's death and thus the centrality of the cross in God's redemptive plan, he is at odds with evangelical accounts of the person and work of Christ. Boff wants to emphasize the criminal character of Jesus's death. For him, Jesus's assassins were criminals

---

66. Grudem, *Systematic Theology*, 582.
67. McClendon Jr., *Doctrine*, 213–37.
68. Oden, *Classic Christianity*, 396.
69. Ibid., 428.
70. Kirk, *Liberation Theology*, 195.

who willingly killed Jesus because of the danger he posed to their religious-political objectives. It seems that Boff's resistance to a theology that holds God's sovereignty and human responsibility in tension is central to his negation of the necessity of Jesus's death. His concern with the sacramentalization of suffering seems to be that ascribing a positive function to suffering would leave the door open to the possibility of using that image in socially oppressive ways. He then denies the necessity of Jesus's death, as his concern is primarily with social transformation rather than doctrinal soundness. Because Boff seems to be convinced that, in the words of Elizabeth Johnson, "Speech about God shapes the life orientation not only of the corporate faith community but in this matrix guides its individual members as well,"[71] he prefers risking doctrinal soundness to possible misuses of atonement theories that render Jesus's death necessary.

Clearly evangelicals must point out Boff's christological reductionisms. The necessity of Jesus's death is to be upheld if evangelicals are to hold to their insistence on biblicism, conversionism, and crucicentrism. However, Boff's conviction that the death of Jesus was not necessary can be denied without rejecting the rest of his Christology. The kenotic, inclusivist, socially oriented, and from-below approach of Boff does not contradict the necessity of Jesus's death; nor does Boff's use of the *Christus-victor* and moral example theories of the atonement do so. Boff's Christology, which is somewhat representative of the classic liberationist approach, can be seen as compatible with evangelical approaches insofar as his denial of the necessity of Jesus's death is rejected, and as long as Boff's Christology is seen as an important but incomplete christological account. Boff reminds evangelicals of the socio-political aspects of Christology that have been largely neglected; however, he does so at the expense of central biblical teachings about Jesus's death. Evangelicals can learn from Boff's emphasis on the socio-political aspects of Christology without letting go of their convictions regarding Jesus's atoning death.

---

71. Johnson, *She Who Is*, 4.

# 7

# Post-Conservative Evangelical Theology: A Bridge Between Evangelicalism and LALT

HAVING LOOKED AT THE main points of tension between NAEvs and LALT, this piece now turns to post-conservative evangelical theology in order to find out if Evangelicalism can indeed be compatible with liberation theology. As mentioned above, this work argues that evangelical theology and LALT can be articulated in non-contradictory ways. This is possible insofar as a post-conservative approach to evangelical theology is adopted and some aspects of LALT are seen not as denials of evangelical concerns, but as incomplete articulations of theological concepts that can be adopted by evangelicals as true—even if complementation is needed. Such an approach goes beyond the conservative evangelical position that sees LALT as a heresy beneficial to evangelical orthodoxy only as a marginal corrective—as a reminder of the necessity to look harder into what is already part of evangelical theology but has been either forgotten or neglected. The shortcoming of the conservative evangelical approach is that it bars LALT from adding any content to evangelical theology, a characteristic that may stem from the conservative tendency to consider the task of theology as finished. Below, I will present the post-conservative evangelical approach as articulated by one of its main proponents, Baptist theologian Roger Olson. After presenting Olson's understanding of the post-conservative position, I will provide some examples of positive interaction between evangelical theologians and LALT.

Evangelicals and Liberation Revisited

## Roger Olson: The Post-Conservative Approach to Evangelical Theology

### Main Tensions Between Conservative and Post-Conservative Views of Evangelicalism

According to Roger Olson, post-conservative evangelical theology represents an attempt to go beyond the right-left spectrum dictated by Enlightenment modes of thinking and, as such, is not to be understood as part of the "evangelical left."[1] For him, the conservative approach fails to be authentically evangelical because of its insistence on the normative status of the "evangelical tradition," which falls short of elevating Scripture above tradition.[2] Olson defines the conservative evangelical theology that he resists as

> ... the style of doing theology that relies heavily on authoritative tradition and rejects or consciously neglects the critical and constructive tasks of theology except insofar as "critical" means rejecting new formulations and revisionings of beliefs.[3]

The conservative approach has, in Olson's opinion, ten general features.

1. Conservative evangelical theology tends to treat a rigid orthodoxy as the essence of authentic Christian faith and consequently of Evangelicalism.

2. Revelation is primarily propositional in the conservative evangelical approach.

3. Conservative evangelical theologians tend to treat some sort of tradition as a magisterium that defines evangelical identity, a feature that generates unnecessary resistance to new theological thinking that could lead to doctrinal correction.

4. Conservative evangelicals are suspicious of theological construction and "spend a great deal of time and energy patrolling evangelical boundaries."[4]

5. Conservative evangelicals usually view Evangelicalism as a "bounded-set category" where an insider-outsider dynamic is overemphasized.

---

1. Olson, *Reformed and Always Reforming*, 12.
2. Ibid., 17.
3. Ibid., 19.
4. Ibid., 23.

6. Olson's sixth feature is the conservative tendency to consider Evangelicalism smaller than the number of people who claim to be part of the movement.

7. Though conservative evangelicals are influenced by modernity, they are suspicious of both modernity and postmodernity—a feature that points to their tendency toward the absolutization of traditional doctrinal convictions.

8. Another feature that enforces the tendency toward absolutization is the conservative conviction that theology can be done without significantly influenced by history and culture. From this point of view, contextualization is limited to form, while content is somehow metaphysically legitimated.

9. Olson's ninth characteristic of conservative evangelical theology is its predisposition to remain only mildly distinguishable from fundamentalism out of which it arguably grew. Olson qualifies this characteristic in the following way:

> . . . insofar as fundamentalism signals anti-intellectualism, an aversion to critical thinking, and separation from secular society and from Christians affected by secularism and liberalism, most conservative evangelical theologians are not fundamentalists. However, many conservatives share with fundamentalists a tendency toward harsh, polemical rhetoric and angry denunciations or ad hominem arguments when writing about fellow evangelicals with whom they disagree.[5]

For Olson, insofar as conservatives use the term "heretic" uncritically, they are functioning as fundamentalists.

10. The tenth feature of conservative evangelical theology is its fear of liberal theology. Because conservatives fear liberalism, they tend to reject any theology that cannot be easily labeled "liberal" or "conservative."[6]

Olson argues that post-conservative evangelicals attempt to move beyond the above mentioned features of conservative evangelical theology. For him, "[m]ost postconservatives view these features as limiting factors and hindrances." However, there are common features between conservative and post-conservative evangelicals. According to Olson, Bebbington's

---

5. Ibid., 25.
6. Ibid., 26.

four hallmarks of evangelical Christianity define the evangelical identity: that is, biblicism, conversionism, crucicentrism, and activism in evangelism and social action.[7] Olson does, however, add a fifth general characteristic to Bebbington's list, which he describes as respect for "the Great Tradition of Christian Belief."[8] Though conservative evangelicals may argue that such convictions are too broad to properly define Evangelicalism, they are held by both them and their post-conservative counterparts.

For the most part, Olson adopts David Bebbington's and Mark Knoll's definition of the four core convictions of Evangelicalism. In the first place, the term "conversionism" refers to "belief in and experience of a spiritual conversion to Christ by faith irreducible to a ritual of initiation into a church or to merely 'turning over a new leaf.'"[9] Personal decision is central to conversion experiences, and though Olson does not argue that it has a prescribed form, it necessarily involves turning one's life over to Jesus Christ as an expression of inward transformation. Seconldy, by "biblicism" Olson means "commitment to the authority of the Bible in all matters of faith and practice together with special love for the Bible as God's Word containing everything necessary for Christian faith and life."[10] At the same time, and with a great number of respected evangelicals, Olson denies the conservative articulation of the doctrine of inerrancy.

Thirdly, crucicentrism means "piety centered on the cross of Jesus Christ and his atoning death."[11] No specific articulation of Christ's atoning work, however, can be considered as the official evangelical position. In Olson's opinion "What all evangelicals agree about is that Christ's death was more than a moral example—it was the sacrifice for sins needed to make sinners acceptable to God."[12] The fourth central feature of Evangelicalism, namely, activism, is understood as the practice of evangelism and social transformation. Together with Olson's fifth hallmark of Evangelicalism—respect for historic Christian orthodoxy—these general characteristics form the core of the movement. Again, Olson allows for different interpretations and articulations of these principles. Furthermore, as it will be mentioned below, one's disposition toward the "center" of Evangelicalism

---

7. Ibid., 27.
8. Ibid., 45.
9. Olson, "Postconservative Evangelicalism," 170.
10. Ibid., 172.
11. Ibid., 173.
12. Ibid., 175.

## Post-Conservative Evangelical Theology

is as significant as full adherence to any one of these central features in establishing one's status as an evangelical.

Given Olson's criticism of conservative evangelicals, it is no surprise that he defines both what "evangelical theology" is and who can be regarded as an "evangelical theologian" broadly. According to him

> Evangelical theology is theology done by an evangelical theologian, and an evangelical theologian is someone who claims to be evangelical, is regarded as working within the evangelical network, and adheres to David Bebbington's four cardinal features of evangelical faith plus one (respect for the Great Tradition of Christian Belief).[13]

For Olson, a broad definition of Evangelicalism is necessary so that the diversity within Evangelicalism is accounted for and so that the door for reform is left open. This approach differs from the conservative one in a number of ways; however, at a fundamental level, whereas conservatives understand evangelical theology as "a continuation and faithful expression of evangelical orthodoxy,"[14] post-conservatives welcome as true evangelicals people who work "within and from the evangelical movement and who therefore share in its ethos as defined by the five common themes and core commitments."[15]

## Characteristics of Post-Conservative Evangelical Theology

According to Olson, post-conservative evangelicals share six common features. First, they consider the main purpose of revelation to be transformation rather than information. Here the difference between post-conservatives and conservatives is primarily a matter of emphasis as, in Olson's opinion, the latter group tends to value information to the detriment of transformation. For Olson

> The point is that postconservatives worry that conservative theology is too caught up in the idea of cognitive Christianity to the neglect of Christianity as a personally transforming and personally involving relationship, rooted in revelation as God's self-giving by

---

13. Olson, *Reformed and Always Reforming*, 38.
14. Ibid., 44.
15. Ibid.

means of a complex of dramatic actions, including but not limited to communication of truths.[16]

In other words, Olson resists the emphasis given to a particular understanding of propositional revelation, insofar as it neglects personal piety and the mystical, transformational, and narratival aspects of Scripture.

Second, post-conservatives and conservatives view theology differently. Whereas conservatives view theology as "conquest," post-conservatives view it as a "journey." This means that while conservatives tend to see theology as a rigid, well defined body of information, post-conservatives view it as an always-constructive task.[17] The incomplete character of theology is a testament to the theologian's own limitation; it is not because of defective revelation that theological openness is needed, but because openness is required for an authentic acknowledgement of the noetic effects of sin.

The third general feature of post-conservative theology is, according to Olson, "a discomfort and dissatisfaction with the reliance of conservative evangelical theology on Enlightenment and modern modes of thought."[18] Olson argues that evangelical theology must be liberated from its "Enlightenment captivity," and that postmodern philosophy can help in this regard. For him, the main post-conservative concern in relation to the ties between conservative evangelicals and the Enlightenment is

> . . . that conservative foundationalism and propositionalism elevate something alien to revelation above revelation as the criterion of truth, and that Christianity gets reduced to a philosophy, to the extent that these Enlightenment-inspired methods and commitments drive evangelical thinking.[19]

Again, conservative evangelical theology is portrayed here as inadequate because of its uncritical acceptance of foreign concepts—in this case, Enlightenment foundationalist epistemology.

Post-conservatives view the evangelical movement as a centered-set category, not as a bounded-set—this is the fourth feature. The primary concern in this view is not establishing who belongs to the movement, but identifying who is nearer to the center. This center includes Jesus Christ, the gospel, and the five core characteristics mentioned above. According to Olson

16. Ibid., 54–55.
17. Ibid., 55.
18. Ibid., 57.
19. Ibid., 58–59.

## Post-Conservative Evangelical Theology

> People gathered around the center or moving toward it are authentically evangelical; people or institutions moving away from it with their backs turned against it are of questionable evangelical status. But it is not a matter or being "in" or "out" as there is no evangelical magisterium to decide that. Conservatives seem to want such an evangelical magisterium, but what would it look like? There is no evangelical headquarters and no central authentication authority.[20]

This open understanding of the evangelical movement, however, does not mean that "everything goes." The center functions as the set of ideals and attitudes that gives the movement its core identity. Though there is a high degree of ambiguity in the post-conservative way of identifying who is an evangelical, the fact that post-conservatives are usually comfortable with ambiguity allows them to be inclusive regarding who belongs to the evangelical movement.

Furthermore, it is because Evangelicalism is a centered-set that it is a movement and not an organization. Movements cannot have boundaries, because boundaries are institutionalizing features; and whenever institutionalization happens, movements transform into organizations—they lose their fluidity and dynamism. For Olson, therefore, one can only call Evangelicalism a movement. He argues that

> Attempts to put boundaries around it appear silly if not disingenuous. As a movement is has certain features, and the main one—the one that identifies it as a movement—is a common center core. Exactly what the center or core is may be debatable. But if there were none, it would not be a movement. Everyone knows, however, that it is a movement.[21]

What is at stake in defining Evangelicalism as a centered-set is not only the possibility of including the variety of evangelical expression, but also the status of Evangelicalism as a movement.

The fifth feature of post-conservative evangelical theology in Olson's judgment is, "a tendency to view the enduring essence of Christianity, and therefore the core identity of evangelical faith, as spiritual experience rather than as doctrinal belief."[22] Finally, Olson's sixth common feature of post-conservative Evangelicalism is a tendency to respect the Great Tradition of Christian Belief while not giving special authoritative status to any tradi-

---

20. Ibid., 60.
21. Olson, "Postconservative Evangelicalism," 165.
22. Olson, *Reformed and Always Reforming*, 61.

tion. In this view, any and every tradition is subject to revision in light of Scripture.[23]

## Positive Evangelical Responses to LALT: Post-Conservative Moves in Response to the Cry of the Poor

Despite the general evangelical dismissal of LALT, some evangelicals have interacted with the movement positively. Though it might be inappropriate to characterize all evangelicals who responded positively to LALT as post-conservatives, some of these responses show post-conservative tendencies—particularly that of being open to theological construction and doctrinal correction. Evangelicals who interacted with LALT in constructive ways are few in number; nevertheless, that there are some who have ventured to do so evidences and perhaps corroborates an argument for the possible compatibility of LALT and post-conservative Evangelicalism.

### LALT Among Latin American Protestants[24]

Among Latin American evangelicals, the responses to LALT were as ambiguous as those of the North Atlantic. Regarding the negative responses, several factors must be considered; however, two factors stand out:

1. The anti-Catholic posture of some Latin American evangelicals who perceived LALT as a mostly Roman Catholic movement.

2. The influence of the American evangelical theology which was disseminated by means of translated literature and/or influential anti-socialist American seminary professors and missionaries who taught and ministered in Latin America.

Theologian Samuel Escobar argues that the fact that Latin American Protestants were always in the minority and thus never significantly involved in the political process was also a factor in their uninvolvement in the populist liberationist movements. According to Escobar, Latin American Protestantism

---

23. Ibid., 64.

24. In Latin America the terms "Protestants" and "evangelicals" are, for the most part, used interchangeably.

. . . has many times experienced oppression from the Catholic majority, has very seldom shared political power at the decision making level, and has never been tempted to align itself with whatever force challenged the politico-religious status-quo.[25]

Escobar seems to be convinced that the historical position of Latin American Protestantism is, in liberationist terms, one that emphasizes denunciation rather than annunciation. Nevertheless, time has shown that if this is true, the general uninvolvement of Latin American Protestants in politics was due to lack of opportunity rather than interest. As Protestantism in general and Pentecostalism in particular secures a bigger share in the religious market, Latin American Protestants are becoming increasingly involved in politics—both by way of electing officials who belong to Protestant and Pentecostal denominations and through political pressure.

It is also important to note the diversity of Evangelicalism in Latin America. In an attempt to simplify such diversity for the sake of analysis, Escobar helpfully divides Latin American Protestantism into three basic categories: transplanted churches, missionary Protestantism, and Pentecostal Protestantism. The first category—transplanted Protestantism—is comprised of churches that came at different moments with European migrants, most of whom did not intend to propagate their beliefs among the native population.[26] Second, missionary Protestantism resulted from two kinds of international evangelistic activity: (1) the missionary work of mainline Protestant churches, which later developed into national churches; and (2) the work of "faith missions" or new denominations from the United States and Great Britain.[27] Finally, Pentecostal Protestantism also resulted from two movements: (1) the missionary work of Pentecostal churches from other countries, such as the Assembly of God from the US and Swedish Pentecostals; and (2) Latin American revival movements, which is the most dynamic and growing Protestant form of Christianity in Latin America.[28] Considering that each of these categories is diverse in itself, it is no surprise that Latin American evangelicals have given diverse responses to LALT.

Despite the fact that, as we have seen above, LALT arguably started within the evangelical movement, it quickly became a primarily Roman Catholic movement and therefore encountered some resistance from Latin

25. Escobar, "Beyond Liberation," 110.
26. Escobar, "A Missiological," 162.
27. Ibid., 162–63.
28. Ibid., 163.

American evangelicals. Nevertheless, the responses to LALT range from open acceptance to complete rejection. Writing in the end of the twentieth century, Pablo Moreno argued that South American Baptists, one of the biggest Protestant denominations in Latin America, have generally responded negatively to LALT. Those within the Baptist denominations who were perceived as supporters of liberation theology were sanctioned by denominational authorities, only to suffer denominational marginalization.[29] According to Moreno. "[t]he general response to Liberation Theology among Baptists (in South America) was one of ignorance or simplifications and a priori accusations."[30] However, Baptists had a different approach to LALT in Central America. Moreno affirms that among Central American Baptists, ". . . the relationship with Liberation Theology was productive and dynamic."[31] Religious educational institutions such as the Latin American Biblical Seminary in Costa Rica, started placing equal weight in the study of the social sciences developed within liberationist-Marxist categories and biblical exegesis—largely due to the dissatisfaction of students with imported hermeneutical methods.[32]

Moreover, Jorge Pixley, who lived and worked among Latin Americans for a long time, points to the Baptist Seminary of Mexico as an example of positive interaction between Latin American evangelicals and LALT. Pixley indicates that, in 1972, the seminary was declared by its rector, Augusto Cotto, to be an open advocate of LALT. Furthermore, influential liberation theologians Porfirio Miranda (author of books such as "Marx and the Bible" and "Communism in the Bible") and Gilberto Gimenez were invited to teach there.[33] Therefore, precedence of full-fledge acceptance of LALT by evangelicals can be found in Latin America—though of course conservative evangelicals who are tempted to enforce imaginary boundaries may claim that any evangelical who accepts LALT should no longer be considered part of the movement.

Sharon Heaney, who dialogues mainly with the theologies of Rene Padilla, Samuel Escobar, and Orlando Costas, argues that Latin American evangelicals generally agree with LALT—despite the fact that they are

---

29. Moreno, "Baptists and Liberation," 74.
30. Ibid., 76.
31. Ibid.
32. Rutschman, "Latin American Liberation," 45.
33. Pixley, "Baptists and Liberation," 59.

critical of the liberationist use of Scripture.³⁴ When assessing the distinctions between LALT and evangelical theology, Heaney criticizes LALT—not because of any flagrant "heresy" she finds in it, but because of what she sees as a few omissions in the liberationist approach. For Heaney, LALT lacks a satisfactory articulation of the consequences of individual sin, the role of the Holy Spirit and of Scripture in the salvation process, and the doctrine of conversion and new birth.

One of the characteristics of LALT that Rene Padilla accepts is Leonardo Boff's ecclesiology. Commenting on the liberationist ecclesiology of Boff, Padilla argues that

> From the perspective of an evangelical theologian, it is quite impossible to go beyond this vision of the church in its internal relationships and its relationship to the world. The ecclesiology of the CEBs has its roots in the New Testament and projects a model that is quite coherent with its teachings regarding what God wants of the church as the firstfruits of the new humanity, the sign and agent of the kingdom, the community in which God's purpose to unite all things under the lordship of Christ is made visible.³⁵

Samuel Escobar also praises the ecclesiological developments made possible by the contributions of LALT. As a matter of fact, Escobar argues that CELAM II brought three renewals to Latin American Christianity:

1. A renewal in the understanding of being the church.
2. A renewal in the understanding of the message of the church.
3. A renewal in the church's missionary method.³⁶

First, Escobar celebrates the emphasis on institutional self-criticism brought by LALT. For him, there is value in being suspicious of the intentions and authenticity of religious institutions. This new understanding of being the church brings not only the awareness of the need for institutional suspicion but also the need for explicit institutional positioning. Escobar argues that this new awareness is a call for theologians to

> . . . do theology from the perspective of the poor, to adopt their own vision of those who are oppressed in society. It is a call to

---

34. Heaney, *Contextual*, 91.
35. Padilla, "The Future of Christianity," 110.
36. Escobar, *Changing Tides*, 65–74.

adopt the vision from the underside of history and to read God's word from that perspective.[37]

Here, Escobar seems to accept not only Boff's ecclesiology and the general liberationist suspicion toward religious institutions, but also the liberationist conviction that hermeneutic endeavors are necessarily partial and that such partiality must be acknowledged.

The emphasis on the need of the Bible for the proper execution of the church's mission was another positive development brought by CELAM II. According to Escobar, though evangelicals were already bible-centered, the move toward an emphasis on the need for the Bible among Catholics after CELAM II helped the Latin American church realize the importance of Scripture. Because the Catholic Church was more organized, influential, and effective than Protestants, their contribution in the process of disseminating the importance of Scripture was invaluable. Talking about this phenomenon, Escobar says that

> The existence of specialized missionary orders in the Catholic Church provided avenues for implementation of new convictions about the importance of scripture. Orders such as the Daughters of St. Paul and the Divine Word Missionaries have provided the infrastructure and personnel for publishing and distributing Bible commentaries studies and expositions at a rate and quality that Protestants find hard to match. The United Bible Societies continue to be an interdenominational and now interconfessional effort with which most Latin American Protestants and many Catholics cooperate for translation, publication, distribution, and use of scripture.[38]

Escobar seems to be convinced that such cooperative efforts, which were many times led by Catholics, were possible in Latin America only because of the developments brought by Catholic liberationists. Furthermore, Escobar praises Catholics for producing more literature and being more rigorous with the quality of their work than Protestants.[39]

The third renewal made possible by CELAM II is, according to Escobar, a renewal in pastoral activity. Escobar agrees with the liberationists when it comes to the preferential option for the poor. For him, the direction of pastoral activity must be guided by the needs of the "least of these." For

37. Ibid., 68–69.
38. Ibid., 71.
39. Ibid.

## Post-Conservative Evangelical Theology

Escobar, this means that, LALT, because of its anti-hierarchical, populist bent moves Catholics closer to Protestants. He once again points to Boff's ecclesiology as an example of a proper ecclesiology—an ecclesiology that resembles Luther's teaching of the "priesthood of all believers."[40]

Orlando Costas, whose influence in Latin American evangelical circles together with that of Padilla and Escobar is highly significant, agrees with LALT's emphasis on the qualitative dimension of salvation. Writing about salvation as justification and liberation, Costas says that

> We know that liberation is "evangelical" when it tears down the structures that perpetuate division among peoples, among men, women, and children, and between the human family and nature –divisions that promote hate, hostility, and resentment, instead of love, well-being, and freedom. Every moment that dignifies human life, that promotes equitable economic relations, and that encourages solidarity among individuals and peoples can be said to be, therefore, a manifestation of the saving power of the gospel.[41]

Being an evangelical, Costas does not think that the only dimension of salvation is the qualitative; no serious liberation theologian does so either. Costas also agrees with most liberationists that the personal dimension of faith is not as important as the social. He asks the question: "Is not the personal dimension of faith equally worthy (to the political dimension) of theological inquiry?" To which he answers: "From a biblical perspective the answer is No, and most liberation theologians would concur."[42]

The examples mentioned above are in no way exhaustive of the Latin American evangelical approach. However, they show not only that LALT was fully accepted within some Latin American evangelical circles but also that three of the most influential Latin American evangelical theologians interacted constructively with it. The dialogue between Padilla, Escobar, and Costas and LALT goes beyond the above mentioned examples; nevertheless, the examples chosen here show that Latin American evangelical theologians use a variety of liberationist theological contributions in the construction of their own theologies.

---

40. Ibid., 74.
41. Costas, *Christ Outside the Gate*, 30.
42. Ibid., 129.

Evangelicals and Liberation Revisited

## Positive North Atlantic Evangelical Responses to LALT

In the North Atlantic, the evangelical responses to LALT were also diverse. Unlike the case of Latin America, North Atlantic evangelicals in general and American evangelicals in particular have been more reserved in their endorsement of the liberationist characteristics they support. Nevertheless, a few North Atlantic evangelical theologians have found value in the theological developments either brought or supported by LALT.

Ronald Sider, for instance, openly supports liberationist concepts such as the "preferential option for the poor" and the equivalency between knowing God and doing justice.[43] Yale theologian Miroslav Volf and LALT share common ground in regards to the political role of religion. For Volf, religions must be free to get involved into politics, and Christianity, in order to fulfill its *telos*, must be transformational. This is so, Volf asserts, because Christianity is a prophetic religion, and the goal of prophetic religions is "to transform the world in God's name rather than to flee from the world into God's arms as do mystical religions."[44] For Volf, when Christianity ceases being prophetic and transformative, when it stops denouncing and announcing, it malfunctions.

Clark Pinnock is another evangelical theologian who calls evangelicals to engage with LALT constructively. In Pinnock's perspective, "It would be good for evangelicals to become informed about the theology of liberation and allow this perspective to challenge our own."[45] He also accepts the liberationist argument that Western Evangelicalism is not apolitical, but sides with the capitalist system. Pinnock says that ". . . when we in North America accept the comfortable alliance between the Gospel and the 'free enterprise system,' we are also taking a political stand ourselves."[46] In an even stronger statement of the political position of North American evangelicals in general, Pinnock argues that they ". . . have come to identify with the interest of the ruling classes and the established order."[47] For Pinnock, North American Evangelicalism needs to be liberated from its bondage to Mammon. In order for this liberation to come, LALT needs to be critically

---

43. Sider, "An Evangelical," 314–17.
44. Volf, *A Public Faith*, x–7.
45. Pinnock, "Liberation Theology," 390.
46. Ibid.
47. Pinnock, "A Call," 135.

appropriated as God's purifying instrument—an instrument that will help North American evangelicals put human needs before profits.[48]

Roger Olson also has shown significant support for the liberationist approach. Olson is critical of some aspects of LALT, but he seems to acknowledge that his criticism is at least partially due to his social location. In one of Olson's latest reflections on LALT, he says that

> I am not a liberation theologian because I am not a member of an oppressed group. But if I were a citizen of certain Latin American or African or Asian countries I very well might be a liberation theologian. Here I can only give them verbal support insofar as they are speaking out on behalf of justice for the poor and oppressed. That does not mean giving them unqualified support with regard to everything they say or do. But, then, I don't give that to any human movement.[49]

It is hard to find a clearer support of LALT coming from an American evangelical scholar. Implicit in Olson's statement seems to be the conviction that at least certain articulations of LALT are proper Christian responses to a specific context—the context of oppression and exploitation of the so called "developing nations." Given Olson's strong evangelical convictions, it seems reasonable to infer that he sees no necessary contradiction between LALT and evangelical theology.

## Post-Conservative Evangelical Responses to LALT: What Can Be Learned From Them?

Post-Conservative evangelical theology is, as seen above, an approach to Evangelicalism that is broad enough to include the diversity of evangelical expressions while at the same time avoiding ambiguity to the point of forfeiting any distinctive identity. Nevertheless, Evangelicalism has no pope, no boundaries, no magisterium; instead, it is characterized by a center that features conversionism, biblicism, crucicentrism, activism, and general respect for the Great Tradition. In such an approach, one's disposition plays a major role in identifying one's status as an evangelical. If an individual is being drawn by the center, he or she is likely to be an evangelical. Christians who are moving away from it, however, may have their status as

---

48. Ibid., 129–32.
49. Olson, "Liberation," lines 55–60.

evangelicals questioned. One cannot help but wonder, however—especially taking into consideration the perception of Evangelicalism by the general population—if anyone who is not an evangelical would ever claim to be one.

Olson's argument that the Post-Conservative approach to Evangelicalism is better than previous and recent attempts to define clear boundaries for the movement may be enough for some to be convinced that Evangelicalism and LALT are not incompatible. Given the openness of Olson's approach, one can argue that if a given liberationist has a disposition toward the evangelical center and thinks of himself or herself as an evangelical, he or she may be properly called an evangelical. Nevertheless, one can anticipate that some will object to that and argue that LALT is still too far from the evangelical center. The examples given above were partially aimed at answering such an objection. Though I will come back to the issue of the compatibility between Evangelicalism and LALT in the concluding chapter, I believe that the positive responses given by evangelicals to LALT already show a move toward the possible compatibility between the two approaches.

In general terms, the positive evangelical responses to LALT can be divided in three categories:

1. LALT as a non-appropriated corrective.
2. Partial acceptance of LALT.
3. LALT as a non-contradictory theological approach.

The first position is taken by those who believe that no theological content of LALT needs to be appropriated by evangelical theologians because the correct aspects of LALT (e.g. the need for focusing on orthopraxis, the call for action against poverty, the partiality of hermeneutics, etc...) are already present in evangelical theology itself. Thus, the sole contribution of LALT is to remind evangelicals how they have stopped being truly evangelical. This is the stance of those who, as mentioned in previous chapters, claim to accept LALT's goals but not its strategies.

The second position—partial acceptance of LALT—is held by those who have appropriated some claims made by liberationists but who still deem that certain aspects of LALT are incompatible with Evangelicalism. Ironically, while some evangelicals accept certain aspects of LALT others don't and, consequently, while some evangelicals deny some aspects of LALT as incompatible with Evangelicalism, others do not. For instance,

## Post-Conservative Evangelical Theology

Sider agrees with the liberationist argument that knowing God is the equivalent of doing God's will, which is justice.[50] Padilla, however, is concerned with this position because, according to him, the belief content of the faith should be emphasized if pragmatism is to be resisted. Padilla argues that "[i]f there is no norm for evaluating praxis itself, sheer utility will provide the only grounds for its justification—the end will justify the means."[51] In Padilla's view, the criterion for discerning God's will, is the cognitive content of the faith, which, consequentially—instead of being equated to—must take precedence over the praxiological element. While Andrew Kirk agrees with Padilla on this issue, Orlando Costas does not. He argues that such an approach "could make praxis a referent to theological reflection rather than its privileged place."[52]

Padilla is also concerned with what he sees as LALT's use of Marxism. He argues that liberation theologians have "fallen prey to a humanist illusion that is not in agreement with either the historical facts or biblical revelation."[53] This issue does not seem to bother Canadian theologian Clark Pinnock. Addressing the issue of the use of Marxism by liberation theologians, Pinnock writes that:

> . . . these theologians do not understand their endorsement of the socialist viewpoint as a betrayal of the Christian faith; they consider it simply an honest description of economic realities, as they see them, and they are surely entitled to the political standpoint they find plausible even if it goes against our own. [. . .] Nor can these theologians be charged with adopting Marxism uncritically; there is evidence throughout their writings of a very profound comprehension of the issues involved.[54]

Pinnock not only thinks that the use of Marxism by LALT is appropriate but, considering the context in which he writes, he also seems to have been convinced by some form of dependency theory, a theory from which liberationists would later distance themselves. Pinnock argues that

> In almost every LA country, a rich and privileged ruling elite, supported by the US and its multinational corporations, holds all the power and is most responsible for the exploitation of the people.

50. Sider, "An Evangelical," 314–17.
51. Padilla, "Liberation Theology: An Evaluation," 15.
52. Costas, *Christ Outside the Gate*, 131.
53. Padilla, "Liberation Theology: An Appraisal," 45.
54. Pinnock, "Liberation Theology," 389–90.

> Indeed, the capitalistic system operating in the 'free world' today, responsive as it is to profit above all, will never, in their opinion, voluntarily give priority to the need of the poor masses over the wants of the rich. The situation is so deeply resistant of change that nothing short of revolution is likely to alter it.[55]

Clearly Pinnock and Padilla, two evangelicals who responded positively to LALT, disagree on the issue of the use of Marxism in theological reflection.

On the other hand, Padilla's acceptance of certain christological claims made by certain liberationists shows his distance from conventional, Western evangelical Christology. Padilla accepts at least three liberationist christological claims:

1. That the humanity of Jesus must be emphasized so that the social dimensions of the gospel can be seen.
2. That Jesus' death was the historical outcome of his life.
3. That Christians are to follow Christ in his commitment to the transformation of the world.[56]

Though Padilla goes beyond these claims with his Christology and further develops the importance of Christ's atoning death, his acceptance of such claims takes him beyond where many evangelical theologians are willing to go.

The above mentioned examples are by no means exhaustive. The number of disagreements among evangelical theologians on what aspects of LALT can or should be incorporated by evangelicals is considerable. In addition, one must consider that the plurality among liberation theologians themselves makes matters even more complex. For instance, Pinnock's apparent nod toward revolution implies that he agrees with the non-pacifist strand of LALT and, therefore, that he is at odds with pacifist liberationists. Therefore, not only must the disagreements among evangelicals who accept certain aspects of LALT be taken into consideration, but also the diversity among liberationists, as evangelical disagreements on certain issues may parallel liberationist disagreements. This situation adds weight to the argument that considering LALT and evangelical theology to be contradictory is only possible if one sees both movements as bounded sets;

---

55. Ibid., 389.

56. See Rene Padilla, "Christology and Mission in the Two Third Worlds" in *Sharing Jesus in the Two Third Worlds* edited by Vinay Samuel and Chris Sugden (Grand Rapids: Eerdmans, 1983): 79–88.

## Post-Conservative Evangelical Theology

in other words, if they are seen as organizations rather than movements. Furthermore, evangelicals who claim to accept only some aspects of LALT may have a reductionistic view of both LALT and evangelical theology.

The third position, LALT as a non-contradictory approach, is the one for which this piece argues. The examples of the Baptist Theological Seminary of Mexico and Olson's qualified openness to the movement seem to be clear representations of this position. To say that LALT does not necessarily contradict evangelical theology, however, is not to dismiss the potential for evangelical theology to complement some aspects of LALT. It is clear that, from an evangelical perspective, LALT not only complements evangelical theology but also needs to be complemented by it. However, outlining such complements in an exhaustive manner is not the focus of this work. The concern here is primarily to show that Evangelicalism and LALT are not necessarily contradictory and, therefore, that it is possible to be both an evangelical and a liberationist.

# 8

# Conclusion

THE ABOVE ATTEMPTS TO bridge the perceived gaps that would render Evangelicalism and LALT contradictory movements focused primarily, though not exclusively, on the diversity in and development of both movements. Because Evangelicalism was defined as a movement that has as its center the features of biblicism, conversionism, crucicentrism, activism, and general respect for historic Christian teaching, it was these features, particularly the first four, on which focus was placed. After introducing the reason for revisiting the evangelical-liberationist interaction—namely, the narrowness with which evangelicals in general responded to LALT—and giving a brief historical overview of the two movements, the liberationist-evangelical interaction was examined by focusing on each of the four hallmarks of Evangelicalism identified by Bebbington and ascribed to the center of the movement by Olson.

## LALT and the Evangelical Hallmarks

### Biblicism

In Chapter 3, I dealt with the issue of biblicism. There it was argued that evangelicals in general, because of their insistence on doctrines such as inerrancy and perspicuity, take issue with the liberationist use of Scripture and hermeneutics which acknowledges the determinant role of context in the process of biblical interpretation. The issue of pervasive interpretive pluralism raised by Christian Smith was used to challenge the general evangelical approach to Scripture and hermeneutics, as it raises questions

## Conclusion

regarding the validity of any hermeneutic that claims metaphysical legitimation. In light of the inability of evangelicals in general to provide a satisfactory answer to the challenges brought to their hermeneutic method by both LALT and pervasive interpretive pluralism, it was argued that the liberationist position of giving context a determinative role in the hermeneutical process is warranted. Therefore, insofar as "biblicism" is defined as the general conservative evangelical approach to the use of Scripture and hermeneutics, Evangelicalism and LALT are irreconcilable.

However, if by "biblicism" one means, as Olson does, "commitment to the authority of the Bible in all matters of faith and practice together with special love for the Bible as God's Word containing everything necessary for faith and life,"[1] the irreconcilability between evangelicals and liberationists ceases to be necessary. Though liberationists in general do not accept unmediated knowledge of Scripture, they do privilege faithfulness to the God that is most clearly revealed in the Bible. Typically liberationist teachings such as the preferential option for the poor, living a life of self-giving to the Other, and the affirmation that to know God is to do justice are articulated in terms of biblical interpretation. Liberationists claim that these teachings among others are central biblical themes rather than mere sociologically-identified needs. Of course liberationists do not think that the Bible answers every question posed by our contemporary situation and, consequently, affirm that interdisciplinarity is indispensable. However, when Olson says that the Bible contains "everything for faith and life"[2] one hardly imagines that he has in mind definitive proof texts for decision-making on highly-specific issues in the fields of bioethics, social policy, and international relations.

Furthermore, Latin American evangelicals such as Samuel Escobar commend the liberationist movement for its indispensable role in raising the continent's biblical literacy rate. As it has been suggested, one of the reasons for the decline of the CEBs and consequently the success of Neo-Pentecostalism was the liberationist insistence on the necessity of reading the Bible, which is a considerable challenge in poor, illiterate communities. Therefore, if "biblicism" is understood in Olson's post-conservative terms, which emphasize the centrality of and love for Scripture instead of rigid interpretations or discredited convictions, the tension between evangelicals and liberationists can be considered significantly diminished.

---

1. Olson, "Postconservative Evangelicalism," 170.
2. Ibid.

Evangelicals and Liberation Revisited

Activism

The issue of activism—particularly social activism—was the focus of chapter 4. When it comes to social activism, for LALT the issue is not so much engagement so much as the forms of social activism it advocates. Chapter 4 focused primarily on the most controversial issues between Evangelicalism and LALT concerning social activism. There it was argued that the conservative evangelical criticism of LALT's articulation of social involvement focuses mainly on the liberationist use of Marx's social analysis, on the socialist nature of the movement, and on the liberationist endorsement of revolutionary violence. As was shown, despite the fact that there are evangelical theologians who identify with the socialist tendencies of LALT, the tendency of conservative evangelicals has been to misrepresent the relationship between LALT and Marxism. Possibly under the influence of Ratzinger's own misrepresentation, which confused the shortcomings of populist movements that were influenced by LALT with LALT itself, conservative evangelicals wrongly characterized the movement as being captive of Marxist ideology.

Furthermore, capitalist evangelicals heavily criticized LALT for its commitments to socialism. Some North Atlantic evangelicals argued that because of its socialist leanings, LALT does a disservice to its own people; for these evangelicals believe that socialism is an ineffective tool in the struggle against poverty. Finally, evangelicals criticized LALT's endorsement of revolutionary violence mainly because of their prioritization of order before justice.

This study demonstrates that even liberation theologians that use Marx's social analysis—though never overly beholden to it—have become increasingly critical of and nuanced regarding the actual benefits of such tools. Rupture with the market system is no longer a necessary characteristic of the movement. The example of liberationist Jung Mo Sung was offered to represent a more balanced attitude toward economic theory, as Jung developed theological approaches to economic issues that argue for the necessity of wealth generation without the flagrant idolatry of the capitalist approach. Finally, the case was made that even given the the legitimation of violence articulated by just war theory, on which non-pacifist conservative evangelicals tend to rely, the liberationist concept of revolution—though no longer often used—can be justified.

While with respect to the issue of social activism liberationists have generally been more active than evangelicals, this piece attempted to show that the form in which LALT usually expresses its social activism is warranted. The changes in the Latin American context have shaped LALT into

*Conclusion*

a more nuanced movement regarding its use of Marx's social analysis, its articulation of socialism, and even its now infrequent call for revolutionary violence. These changes have brought Evangelicalism and LALT closer together today, as greater common ground has been established for dialogue between conservative North Atlantic evangelicals and liberationists about socio-political solutions to the problem of poverty. Of course, just as Democrat and Republican evangelicals are able to disagree without forgoing their common evangelical identity, so too conservative North Atlantic evangelicals and liberationists share a commitment to social activism while not seeing eye to eye on most socio-political issues; for, particularly with regard to social form, liberationists are as close to what post-conservatives call "the evangelical center" as anyone else.

## Conversionism

The issue of conversionism was treated in chapter 5. This issue appeared in connection with two specific theologians, namely, James McClendon, Jr. and Gustavo Gutierrez. Conversionism, which is directly related to a specific articulation of soteriology, is defined by Olson as "belief in and experience of a spiritual conversion to Christ by faith not reduced to a ritual of initiation into a church or merely 'turning over a new leaf.'"[3] Though liberationists do not necessarily deny this particular affirmation of conversionism and, therefore, are open to an "evangelical" salvation experience, this articulation of conversionism tends to emphasize the eschatological rather than the social dimension of salvation. When speaking of conversion, liberationists want to emphasize the need for converting to the Other. For them, in order for salvation to be integral, it must also include a praxiological element, as salvation also comes by way of one's commitment to the poor in their struggle for a just society. Preaching the necessity of eschatological salvation without being committed to social transformation is, in the liberationist mind, tantamount to proclaiming a false gospel. Consequently, accepting an articulation of a purely eschatological salvation is accepting a deficient message of salvation.

Therefore, the issue that liberationists may have with the evangelical hallmark of conversionism is not what it affirms, but what it fails to make explicit—namely, that conversion to Christ without conversion to the Other is an incomplete conversion and, as such, needs further fulfillment.

3. Ibid.

Moreover, because LALT is an inclusivist theology, it also affirms that wherever the gospel has not been authentically preached, conversion to the Other serves as evidence of an affirmative response to God's call in one's conscience. Those who are inculpably ignorant, therefore, must still undergo a conversion in order to be in right standing with God—despite the fact that such conversion is not explicitly Christian.

## Crucicentrism

LALT is criticized by many evangelicals for not giving a central place to the cross; chapter 6 was a modest attempt to challenge such criticism. Olson defines crucicentrism as "piety centered on the cross of Jesus Christ and his atoning death."[4] Though liberationists may affirm such a statement, focusing on following Jesus's example of living his life for the sake of the Other is, as was shown in chapter 6, what they want to emphasize. There is no necessary contradiction between the two affirmations, but if either the evangelical or the liberationist emphasis is affirmed by itself, it will be considered incomplete by one persuasion or the other.

## LALT and Other Post-Conservative Evangelical Characteristics

In addition to the fact that LALT can be articulated in ways that do not contradict the central features of Evangelicalism, it also shares other features with post-conservative evangelical theology. First, as with post-conservative evangelical theology, LALT emphasizes revelation as having a primarily transformational rather than informative function. The fact that liberationists usually see theological reflection as being secondary to the commitment to transformative praxis for which God calls them is evidence for the strong presence of this characteristic in LALT. Second, liberationists see theology as an always-constructive task. In fact this is a characteristic not only of LALT but also of many professing contextual theologies. In the case of LALT, this characteristic is made evident by its adaptation to new socio-economic-cultural realities and its willingness to replace old social theories with new ones. As reality is perceived differently by new readings of the "signs of time," new solutions are proposed and old, unproven

---

4. Ibid., 173.

strategies are unashamedly left behind. Liberation theologians are usually unafraid of taking risks. As mentioned above, irrelevance is their worst fear—not an imaginary magisterium.

Another common characteristic between LALT and post-conservative Evangelicalism is their proclivity to include those who claim to belong to their movements. Though LALT was never homogeneous, discussions about who did or did not belong to it were never a significant part of its agenda. As in the case of post-conservative Evangelicalism, this means that LALT can be better described as a centered-set rather than a bounded-set movement. As was argued above, features such as Marxism, endorsement of revolutionary violence, Roman Catholicism, and rupture with the market system—which are usually identified as the convictional boundaries that define LALT—are not only unnecessary to it but also rarely found together in the theologies of major liberationists. The general characteristics that define the center of LALT more appropriately are:

1. The praxis of the liberation of the poor.
2. The acknowledgement of the necessity of a scientific analysis of social reality.
3. The conscience of the socio-economic dependence of theology and of the church.
4. The understanding of theological reflection as a tool for social transformation.
5. The central place of economy in theological reflection.[5]

This is because they respect the diversity within the movement. None of these characteristics necessarily conflict with Bebbington's hallmarks of Evangelicalism or with Olson's addition to Bebbignton's list.

Giving greater importance to spiritual experience than to doctrinal belief is another common feature of these two theologies. Theologians such as Boff and Gutierrez affirm that it is spiritual experience that gives rise to theology. Finally, a tendency to respect the Great Tradition of Christian belief is also shared between post-conservative evangelicals and liberationists in general. In contrast, though characteristics such as the "epistemological break" may be understood as a post-modern move made by liberationists, they are usually suspicious of what they perceive as post-modernity's tendency toward giving up on the great historical projects. Somewhat

---

5. Ribeiro, *A Teologia*, 29.

surprisingly then, post-conservatives are more comfortable than liberation theologians with post-modern philosophy in general.

## Final Observations

There are still many issues to be explored when it comes to the compatibility between LALT and Evangelicalism. A definitive case for such compatibility can only be successfully made in more extensive works that deal with the potential controversies between the two approaches individually. However, a case for the possibility of articulating an evangelical-liberationist approach has been made. Despite the fact that there may still be gaps in the arguments presented above, I am confident that LALT and Evangelicalism are not necessarily contradictory movements, and characterizing them as contradictory is not appropriate if their respective diversity and dynamism is taken into consideration. In a world where structural injustice and impiety run wild, a theological approach that combines the strengths of both Evangelicalism and LALT is more needed than ever.

# Bibliography

Aguilar, Mario I. "The Kairos of Medellin: Towards a Movement for Liberation and New Mission After Vatican II." In *Movement or Moment? Assessing Liberation Theology Fourty Years After Medellin*, edited by Patrick Claffey and Joe Egan, 9–28. Bern: Peter Lang, 2009.

Ahlstrom, Sydney E. "The Radical Turn in Theology and Ethics: Why it Ocurred in the 60s." *Annals of the American Academy of Political and Social Science* 387 (1970) 1–13.

Aldunate, José. "La 'Doctrina Social de la Iglesia' Su Historia, Sus Planteamientos, Su Encontro Con la Teología de la Liberación." In *A Esperança dos Pobres Vive: Clonetânea em Homenagem aos 80 Anos de José Comblin*, edited by Paulo Bazaglia, 301–314. São Paulo: Paulus, 2003.

Althaus-Reid, Marcella. *The Queer God*. London: Routledge, 2003.

Armerding, Carl Edwin. "Exodus: The Old Testament Foundation of Liberation." In *Evangelicals and Liberation*, edited by Carl Edwin Armerding, 43–60. Phillipsburg: P & R Publishing, 1977.

Assmann, Hugo, and Jung Mo Sung. *Deus em Nós: O Reinado que Acontece no Amor Solidário aos Pobres*. São Paulo: Paulus, 2010.

Barth, Karl. *Dogmatics in Outline*. New York: Harper & Brothers, 1959.

Bebbington, David. *Evanghelicalism in Modern Britain: The Age of Edwards, Whitefield, and the Wesleys*. Downers Grove: Intervarsity, 2003.

Beeck, Frans Josef Van. *Catholic Identity After Vatican II: Three Types off Faith in One Church*. Chicago: Loyola University Press, 1983.

Beeck, Frans Josef Van. *God Encountered: A Contemporary Systematic Theology 1*. Collegeville: Michael Glazier, 1989.

Bell, Daniel. *Just War as Christian Discipleship: Recentering the Tradition in the Church Rather than the State*. Grand Rapids: Brazos Press, 2009.

Belli, Humberto, and Ronald Nash. *Beyond Liberation Theology*. Grand Rapids: Baker Book House, 1992.

Benson, Bruce Ellis, and Peter Goodwin Heltzel. *Evangelicals and Empire: Christian Alternatives to the Political Status Quo*. Grand Rapids: Brazos, 2008.

Berry, Mary Elizabeth, et al. *Prophetic Evangelicals: Envisioning a Just and Peaceable Kingdom*. Grand Rapids: Wm. B. Eerdmans, 2012.

Berryman, Phillip. "La Generación-Medellín y Sus Sucesores." In *A Esperança dos Pobres Vive: Coletânea em Homenagem aos 80 Anos de José Comblin*, edited by Paulo Bazaglia, 77–88. São Paulo: Paulus, 2003.

# Bibliography

Bevans, Stephen. "Models of Contextual Theology." *Missiology: An International Review* XIII/2 (1985) 185–202.

Boff, Clodovis. *Theology and Praxis: Epistemological Foundations*. Maryknoll: Orbis Books, 1987.

Boff, Leonardo. *Church: Charism and Power. Liberation Theology and the Institutional Church*. New York: Crossroads, 1985.

Boff, Leonardo. *Eclesiogénesis: Las Comunidades de Base Reiventam la Iglesia*. Santander: Sal Terrae, 1980.

Boff, Leonardo. *Jesus Christ Liberator: A Critical Christology for Our Times*. Maryknoll: Orbis Books, 1978.

Boff, Leonardo. "La Iglesia Y la Teologia de la Liberacion." *Cuadernos de Teologia* 6/4 (1985) 95–98.

Boff, Leonardo. "Os Interesses dos Pobres São os Interesses de Deus." *Cuadernos de Teologia* 6/4 (1985) 99–102.

Boff, Leonardo. *Passion of Christ, Passion of the World: The Facts, the Interpretation, and the Meaning for Yesterday and Today*. Maryknoll: Orbis Books, 1987.

Boff, Leonardo. "The Need for Political Saints: From the Spirituality of Liberation to the Practice of Liberation." *Cross Currents* 30/4 (1980) 369–384.

Boff, Leonardo, and Clodovis Boff. *Introducing Liberation Theology*. Maryknoll: Orbis Books, 1987.

Bonino, Jose Miguez. *Doing Theology in a Revolutionary Situation*. Philadelphia: Fortress Press, 1975.

Bonino, Jose Miguez. *Toward a Christian Political Ethics*. Philadelphia: Fortress Press, 1983.

Boyd, Gregory A., and Paul Eddy. *Accross the Spectrum: Understanding Issues in Evangelical Theology*. Grand Rapids: Baker Academic, 2009.

Brown, Harold. "What is Liberation Theology?" In *Liberation Theology*, edited by Ronald Nash, 1-16. Milford: Mott Media, 1984.

Bullivant, Stephen. "Sine Culpa? Vatican II and Inculpable Ignorance." *Theological Studies* 72 (2011) 70–86.

Chaouch, Malik Tahar. "Cristianismo Y Politica en America Latina: El Paradigma de la Teologia de la Liberacion." *Desafios* 17 (2007) 157–199.

Comblin, José. *Quais os Desafios dos Temas Teológicos Atuais?* São Paulo: Paulus, 2007.

Conn, Harvie. "Contextualization: Where Do We Begin?" In *Evangelicals and Liberation*, edited by Carl Edwin Armerding, 90–119. Phillipsburg: P & R Publishing, 1977.

Conn, Harvie. "The Mission of the Church." In *Evangelicals and Liberation*, edited by Carl Edwin Armerding, 60–89. Phillipsburg: P & R Publishing, 1977.

Cook, Michael L. "Jesus From the Other Side of History: Christology in Latin America." *Theological Studies* 44/2 (1983) 258–287.

Costas, Orlando. *Christ Outside the Gate: Mission Beyond Christendom*. Maryknoll: Orbis Books, 1982.

Cox, Harvey. *The Silencing of Leonardo Boff: The Vatican and the Future of World Christianity*. Oak Park: Meyer-Stone, 1988.

Davis, Stephen. "Is Kenosis Orthodox?" In *Exploring Kenotic Christology: The Self-Emptying of God*, edited by C. Stephen Evans, 112–138. Oxford: Oxford University Press, 2006.

Dillenberger, John, and Claude Welch. *Protestant Christianity: Interpreted Through its Development*. New York: Charles Scribner's Sons, 1954.

*Bibliography*

Duffy, Maria. "In No Man's Land: The Option for thePoor and the Crisis of Globalization." In *Movement or Moment? Assessing Liberation Theology Fourty Years After Medellin*, edited by Patrick Claffey and Joe Egan, 125–138. Bern: Peter Lang, 2009.

Dulles, Avery. *Models of the Church*. New York: Image, 2002.

Dussel, Enrique. "Recent Latin American Theology." In *The Church in Latin America*, edited by Enrique Dussel, 391–402. Maryknoll: Orbis Books, 1992.

Escobar, Samuel. "A Missiological Approach to Latin American Protestantism." *International Review of Mission* (April 1998) 161–173.

Escobar, Samuel. "Beyond Liberation Theology: Evangelical Missiology in Latin America." *International Bulletin of Missionary Research* 6/3 (1982) 108–114.

Escobar, Samuel. *Changing Tides: Latin America and World Mission Today*. Maryknoll: Orbis Books, 2002.

Escobar, Samuel. *La Fe Evangelica y las Teologias de la Liberacion*. El Passo: Casa Bautista de Publicaciones, 1987.

Escobar, Samuel, and John Driver. *Christian Mission and Social Justice*. Scottdale: Herald Press, 1978.

Fraassen, Bas C. "The False Hopes of Traditional Epistemology." *Philosophy and Phenomenological Research* 60/2 (2000) 253–280.

Froese, Paul. *The Plot to Kill God: Fidings From the Soviet Experiment on Seculatization*. Berkley: University of California Press, 2008.

Gibson, David. "Who Needs a Lifetime?" No Pages. Online: http://www.thetablet.co.uk/article/12086.

Gooren, Henri. "Catholic and Non-Catholic Theologiesof Liberation: Poverty, Sef-Improvement, and Ethics Among Small-Scale Entrepreneurs in Guatemala City." *Journal for the Scientific Study of Religion* 41/1 (2002) 29–45.

Gorringe, Tom. "Political Readings of Scripture." In *The Cambridge Companion to Biblical Interpretation*, edited by John Barton, 67–80. Cambridge; New York: Cambridge University Press, 1998.

Grenz, Staney, and Roger Olson. *20th Century Theology: God & the World in a Transitional Age*. Downers Grove: Inter Varsity Press, 1992.

Grudem, Wayne. *Systematic Theology*. Grand Rapids: Zondervan, 1994.

Gutierrez, Gustavo. *A Theology of Liberation (1st ed.)*. Maryknoll: Orbis Books, 1973.

Gutierrez, Gustavo. *A Theology of Liberation: History, Politics, and Salvation*. Maryknoll: Orbis Books, 1988.

Gutierrez, Gustavo. "Apuntes Para Una Teologia de la Liberacion." In *Religion, Instrumento de Liberacion?*, edited by Gustavo Gutierrez, et al., 23–76. Madrid: Edicion Marova, 1973.

Gutierrez, Gustavo. *On Job: God-Talk and the Suffering of the Innocent*. Maryknoll: Orbis Books, 1987.

Gutierrez, Gustavo. "The Church and the Poor: A Latin American Perspective." In *The Reception of Vatican II*, edited by Giuseppe Alberigo et al., 171–193. Washington: The Catholic University of the America, 1987.

Gutierrez, Gustavo. *The God of Life*. Maryknoll : Orbis Books, 1991.

Gutierrez, Gustavo. *We Drink from our Own Wells: The Spiritual Journey of a People*. Maryknoll: Orbis Books, 1983.

Hamilton, Kenneth. "Liberation Theology: An Overview." In *Evangelicals & Liberation*, edited by Carl Ewald Amerding, 1–9. Phillipsburg: P & R Publishing, 1977.

## Bibliography

Hamilton, Kenneth. "Liberation Theology: Lessons Positive and Negative." In *Evangelicals and Liberation*, edited by Carl Armerding, 120–127. Phillipsburg: P & R Publishing, 1977.

Hauerwas, Stanley. *War and the American Difference: Theological Reflections on Violence and National Identity*. Grand Rapids: Baker Academic, 2011.

Hayek, Friedrich. *Individualism and Economic Order*. Chicago: The University of Chicago Press, 1948.

Heaney, Sharon E. *Contextual Theology for Latin America: Liberation Themes in Evangelical Perspective*. Colorado Springs: Paternoster, 2008.

Hennelly, Alfred T. *Liberation Theology: A Documentary History*. Maryknoll: Orbis Books, 1990.

Hennelly, Alfred T. *Liberation Theologies: The Global Pursuit of Justice*. Mystic: Twenty-Third Publications, 1995.

Henry, Carl F. "Liberation Theology and the Scriptures." In *Liberation Theology*, edited by Ronald Nash, 187–202. Milford: Mott Media, 1984.

Humphreys, Fisher, and Philip Wise. *Fundamentalism*. Macon: Smyth and Helwys, 2004.

Hundley, Raymond C. *Radical Liberation Theology: An Evangelical Response*. Wilmore: Bristol Books, 1987.

Johson, Elizabeth. *She Who Is: The Mystery of God in Feminist Theological Discourse*. New York: Crossroads, 1992.

Kee, Alistair. "The Conservatism of Liberation Theology: Four Questions for Jon Sobrino." *Political Theology* 3 (2000) 30–43.

Kirk, J. Andrew. *Liberation Theology: An Evangelical View of the Third World*. Atlanta: John Knox Press, 1979.

Kung, Hans, and Leonard Swindler (eds.). *Has the Vatican Betrayed Vatican II?* . San Francisco: Harper & Row, 1987.

Lewis, Hannah. *Deaf Liberation Theology*. Burlington: Ashgate, 2007.

Lopes, Augustus Nicodemus. "A Hermanêutica da Teologia da Libertação: Uma Análise de Jesus Cristo Libertador de Leonardo Boff." *Fides Reformata* 3/2 (1998) 1–24.

Mackey, Steven. "Praxis as the Context for Interpretation: A Study of Latin American Liberation Theology." *Journal of Theology for Southern Africa* 24 (1978) 31–43.

Markey, John J. "Praxis in Liberation Theology: Some Clarifications." *Missiology: An International Review* XXIII/2 (1995) 179–195.

Marx, Karl. "Theses on Feuerbach." In *Writtings of the Young Marx on Philosophy and Society*, edited and D. Easton, & Kurt H. Guddat, 400–402. New York: Doubleday, 1967.

McCelndon Jr., James. *Doctrine*. Nashville: Abingdon Press, 1994.

McCLendon Jr., James. *Ethics*. Nashville: Abingdon Press, 2002.

McCormack, Bruce L. "Karl Barth's Christology as a Resource for a Reformed Version of Kenoticism." *International Journal of Systematic Theology* 8/3 (2006) 243–251.

McGovern, Arthur F. *Liberation Theology and Its Critics: Toward an Assessment*. Maryknoll: Orbis Books, 1989.

Melloni, Alberto, and Christoph Theobald 9 (eds.). *Vatican II: A Forgotten Future?* London: SCM Press, 2005.

Miguez, Nestor, et al. *Beyond the Spirit of Empire*. London: SCM Press, 2009.

Moreno, Pablo. "Baptists and Liberation Theology in South America." *Baptist History and Heritage* (Winter 2000) 72–81.

# Bibliography

Moylan, Tom. "Denunciation/Annunciation: The Radical Methodology of Liberation Theology ." *Cultural Critique* 20 (1991-1992) 33–64.
Muskus, Eddy J. *The Origins and Early Development of Liberation Theology in Latin America*. Waynesboro: Paternoster, 2002.
Nash, Ronald. "The Christian Choice Between Capitalism and Socialism." In *Liberation Theology*, edited by Ronald Nash, 45-68. Milford: Mott Media, 1984.
Nessan, Craig L. *Orthopraxis or Heresy?: The North American Theological Response to Latin American Liberation theology*. American Academy of Religion, 1989.
Novak, Michael. *The Spirit of Democratic Capitalism*. Bolder: Madison Books, 1990.
Nunez, Miguel Angel. "Relevancia y Pertinencia Actual de la Teologia de la Liberacion." *DavarLogos* 4/1 (2005) 49–63.
Odem, Thomas C. *Classic Christianity: A Systematic Theology*. New York: Harper Collins, 1992.
O'Donovan, Oliver. *The Just War Revisited*. New York: Cambridge University Press, 2003.
Olson, Roger. "Liberation Theology." No pages. Online: http://www.patheos.com/blogs/rogerolson/2010/10/liberation-theology/
Olson, Roger. "Postconservative Evangelicalism." In *Four Views on the Spectrum of Evangelicalism*, edited by Andrew Naselli and Collin Hansen, 161–187. Grand Rapids: Zondervan, 2011.
Olson, Roger. *Reformed and Always Reforming: The Postconservative Approach to Evangelical Theology*. Grand Rapids: Baker Academic, 2007.
Olson, Roger. "Tensions in Evangelical Theology." *Dialog: A Journal of Theology* 42/1 (2003) 76–85.
Olson, Roger. *The Westminster Handbook to Evangelical Theology*. Louisvile: Westminster-John Knox Press, 2004.
Padilla, Rene. "Christology and Mission in the Two Third Worlds." In *Sharing Jesus in the Two Third Worlds*, edited by Vinay Samuel and Chris Sugden, 79–88. Grand Rapids: Eerdmans, 1983.
Padilla, Rene. "Liberation Theology." *Reformed Journal* 33/6 (1983) 21–23.
Padilla, Rene. "Liberation Theology: An Appraisal." In *Freedom and Discipleship*, edited by Daniel S. Schipani, 34–51. Maryknoll: Orbis Books, 1989.
Padilla, Rene. "Liberation Theology: An Evaluation." *Reformed Journal* 33/7 (1983) 14–18.
Padilla, Rene. "The Future of Christianity in Latin America: Missiological Perspectives and Challenges ." *International Bulletin of Missionaryl Research* 23/3 (1999) 105–112.
Petrella, Ivan. *Beyond Liberation Theology: A Polemic*. London: SCM, 2008.
Petrella, Ivan. "Introduction: Latin American Liberation Theology." In *Latin American Liberation Theology: The Next Generation*, edited by Ivan Petrella, xi–xxii. Maryknoll: Orbis Books, 2005.
Petrella, Ivan. *The Future of Liberation Theology: An Argument and Manifesto*. Burlington: Ashgate Publishing, 2004.
Pettegrew, Larry D. "Liberation Theology and Hermeneutical Preunderstandings." *Bibliotheca Sacra* 148/591 (1991) 274–287.
Phan, Peter. "Method in Liberation Theology." *Theological Studies* 61/1 (2000) 40–63.
Piar, Carlos. *Jesus and Liberation: A Critical Analysis of the Christology of Latin American Liberation Theology*. New York: Peter Lang, 1994.
Pinnock, Clark. "A Call For the Liberation of North American Christians." In *Evangelicals and Liberation*, edited by Carl Edwin Armerding, 128–136. Phillipsburg: P & R Publishing, 1977.

## Bibliography

Pinnock, Clark. "Liberation Theology: The Gains, The Gaps." *Christianity Today* 20/8 (1975): 389–391.

Pixley, Jorge. "Baptists and Liberation Theology: Mexico, Central America, and the Caribbean." *Baptist History and Heritage* 35/1 (2000) 55–71.

Ratzinger, Joseph Cardinal. "Liberation Theology." In *Liberation Theology: A Documentary History*, edited by Alfred T. Hennelly, 367–374. Maryknoll: Orbis Books, 1990.

Rauschenbusch, Walter. *Christianizing the Social Order*. New York: The Macmillan Company, 1915.

Reed, Randall W. *A Clash of Ideologies: Marxism, Liberation Theology, and Apocalypticism in New Testament Studies*. Pickwick Publications: Eugene, 2010.

Ribeiro, Claudio de Oliveira. *A Teologia da Libertação Morreu?: Reino de Deus e Espiritualidade Hoje*. São Paulo: Fonte Editorial, 2010.

Ribeiro, Claudio de Oliveira. "Has Liberation Theology Died? Reflections on the Relationship Between Community Life and the Globalization of The Economic System." *Ecumenical Review* 51/3 (1999) 304–314.

Ribeiro, Claudio de Oliveira. "Teologia é no Plural: Hugo Assmann e a Teologia Latino-Americana da Libertação." *Estudos de Religião* 24/38 (2010) 92–100.

Roberts, W. Dayton. "Where has Liberation Theology Gone Wrong?" *Christianity Today* 23/24 (1979) 1399–1401.

Rutschman, LaVerne A. "Latin American Liberation Theology and Radical Anabaptism." *Journal of Ecumenical Studies* 19/1 (Winter 1992) 38–56.

Segundo, Juan Luiz. *Signs of the Times: Theological Reflections*. Maryknoll: Orbis Books, 1993.

Segundo, Juan Luiz. *The Liberation of Theology*. Maryknoll: Orbis Books, 1976.

Sider, Ronal J. *Rich Christians in an Age of Hunger: Moving from Affluence to Generosity*. Nashville: Thomas Nelson, 2005.

Sider, Ronald J. "An Evangelical Theology of Liberation." *Christian Century* 97/10 (1980) 314–318.

Sider, Ronald J. *Non-Violence: The Invincible Weapon?* Dallas: Word Publishing, 1989.

Sigmund, Paul. *Liberation Theology at the Crossroads: Democracy or Revolution?* New York: Oxford University Press, 1990.

Smith, Christian. *The Bible Made Impossible: Why Biblicism is Not a Truly Evangelical Reading of Scripture*. Grand Rapids: Brazos Press, 2011.

Smith, Christian. *The Emergence of Liberation Theology: Radical Religion and Social Movement Theory*. Chicago: University of Chicago Press, 1991.

Sobrino, Jon. *Christology at the Crossroads: A Latin American Approach*. Maryknoll: Orbis Books, 1978.

Soto, Hernando de. *The Mystery of Capital: Why Capitalism Triumphs in the West and Fails Everywhere Else*. New York: Basic Books, 2000.

Sung, Jung Mo. *Conversando Sobre Ética e Sociedade*. Petrópolis: Editora Vozes, 1995.

Sung, Jung Mo. "Crise das Ideologias, Utopias Secularizadas e o Reino de Deus." *Perspectiva Teologica* 25 (1993) 323–337.

Sung, Jung Mo. *Cristianismo de Libertação: Espiritualidade e Luta Social*. São Paulo: Paulus, 2008.

Sung, Jung Mo. *Desire, Market, and Religion*. London: SCM Press, 2007.

Sung, Jung Mo. *Deus em uma Economia Sem Coração. Neoliberalismo e Pobreza: Desafios à Evangelização*. São Paulo: Paulus, 1992.

Sung, Jung Mo. *Se Deus Existe Porque Há Pobreza?* São Paulo: Paulinas, 1995.

*Bibliography*

Sung, Jung Mo. *Sujeito e Sociedades Complexas: Para Repensar os Horizonted Utópicos.* Petrópolis: Editora Vozes, 2002.
Sung, Jung Mo. *Teologia e Economia: Repensando a Teologia da Libertação e Utopias.* Petrópolis: Editora Vozes, 1994.
Sung, Jung Mo. "The Human Being as Subject." In *Latin American Liberation Theology: The Next Generation*, by Ivan Petrella (edt.), 1-19. Maryknoll: Orbis Books, 2005.
Sweeney, Douglas A. *The American Evangelical Story: A History of the Movement.* Grand Rapids: Baker Academic, 2005.
Tillich, Paul. *Dynamics of Faith.* New York: Harpers & Brothers, 1957.
Tombs, David. *Latin American Liberation Theology.* Boston: Brill Academic Publishers, 2002.
Tombs, David. "Latin American Liberation Theology: Moment, Movement, Legacy." In *Movement or Moment? Assessing Liberation Theology Forty Years After Medellin*, edited by Patrick Claffey and Joe Egan, 29-54. Bern: Peter Lang, 2009.
Torre, Miguel de la (edt). *The Hope of Liberation in World Religions.* Waco: Baylor University Press, 2008.
Torre, Miguel de la. *Doing Christian Ethics from the Margins.* Maryknoll: Orbis Books, 2004.
Torre, Miguel de la. *Latina/o Ethics: Moving Beyond Eurocentric Moral Thinking.* Waco: Baylor University Press, 2010.
Tweed, Thomas A. *Crossing and Dwelling: A Theory of Religion.* Cambridge: Harvard University Press, 2006.
Vinz, Warren L. *Pulpit Politics: Faces of American Protestant Nationalism in the Twenieth Century.* New York: State University of New York Press, 1997.
Volf, Miroslav. *A Public Faith: How Followers of Christ Should Serve the Common Good.* Grand Rapids: Brazos Press, 2011.
Waltermire, Donald E. *The Liberation Christologies of Leonardo Boff and Jon Sobrino: Latin American Contributions to Contemporary Christology.* Lanham: University Press of America, 1994.
Warner, Rob. *Reinventing English Evangelicalism, 1966-2001: A Theological and Sociological Study.* Colorado Springs: Paternoster, 2007.
Witvliet, Theo. *A Place in the Sun: Liberation Theology in the Third World.* Maryknoll: Orbis Books, 1985.
Witvliet, Theo. *The Way of the Black Messiah: The Hermeneutical Challenge of Black Theology as a Theology of Liberation.* Oak Park: Meyer-Stone Books, 1987.
Zizec, Slavoj. *Violence: Six SidewaysReflections.* New York: Picador, 2008.

www.ingramcontent.com/pod-product-compliance
Lightning Source LLC
Chambersburg PA
CBHW071857160426
43197CB00013B/2517